Archaeology
Monograph 4

A Preliminary Bibliography of Early Man in Eastern North America 1839-1973

Compiled by Peter L. Storck
with the assistance of Mima Kapches

Royal Ontario Museum
Publication date: 31 January, 1975
Suggested citation: Arch. Monogr. ROM
ISBN: 0-88854-158-9

Royal Ontario Museum
Publications in Archaeology

The Royal Ontario Museum publishes two series in the field of archaeology: Monographs, a numbered series of original publications, and Papers, a numbered series of primarily shorter original publications. All manuscripts considered for publication are subject to the editorial policies of the Royal Ontario Museum, and to review by persons outside the Museum staff who are authorities in the particular field involved.

Art and Archaeology Editorial Board
Chairman: Walter M. Tovell
Editor: D. M. Pendergast
Associate Editor: Veronika Gervers-Molnar
Associate Editor: E. J. Keall

Peter L. Storck is Assistant Curator in the Office of the Chief Archaeologist, Royal Ontario Museum.

Price: $3.00
© The Royal Ontario Museum, 1975
100 Queen's Park, Toronto, Canada   M5S 2C6
Printed by Brown & Martin Ltd., Kingston, Canada

Contents

Introduction 1
Bibliography 3
Addenda 98
Geographical Index 101
Index of Selected Topics 104
Index of Selected Sites and Localities 107

Introduction

This bibliography contains 1242 titles of abstracts, short comments on single artifacts and small collections, journal articles, reviews, monographs, and books dealing in whole or in part with the subject of Early Man in eastern North America. This project began quite unintentionally several years ago when I started a small card file for the purpose of keeping track of references on the subject of Early Man which I happened upon in the course of casual reading or research, primarily on other topics. Initially, the references were compiled intermittently and unsystematically. Only after collecting some 2000 titles dealing with North America as a whole did it occur to me that the collection might also be useful to others despite the fact that it was certainly not complete. The last bibliographies on the subject were published by E.H. Sellards in 1940 and 1947 and deal with the period up to 1945. Nothing similar has appeared since, and although publications concerned with regional or continental overviews of Early Man provide sometimes rather lengthy lists of references, there is a need for a larger compilation of sources, perhaps appearing periodically as do the various bibliographies on fossil vertebrates and geological research published by the Geological Society of America. Such a project is, of course, beyond the resources of a single individual. Certainly this bibliography, dealing only with Early Man in eastern North America, is not a comprehensive listing of all of the publications on the subject. Such a bibliography would almost certainly contain between 2000 and 3000 titles and possibly more. Although incomplete, this bibliography includes most if not all of the more important and frequently-cited publications on the subject, and will be of use in both teaching and research.

The term Early Man is used here in the broadest possible sense, including not only the various manifestations of early and late Palaeo-Indian cultures, which is the usual meaning of the term, but possible antecedent cultures as well. During the past two decades, re-evaluation of the late 19th and early 20th century reports of "Eolithic" and "Paleolithic" tools as well as some of the more recent evidence for possible Palaeo-Indian antecedents has resulted either in the outright dismissal of the evidence (as in the case of "geofacts" or naturally fractured objects) or in the assignment of the supposed complexes or collections of material to later cultures. While these earlier interpretations no longer warrant serious consideration, the sources have, of course, been included in this bibliography because of their historical interest.

Eastern North America is defined as including those Canadian provinces east of Manitoba (Ontario, Quebec, New Brunswick, Prince Edward Island, Newfoundland, and Nova Scotia) and the United States east of the Mississippi River. Minnesota has also been included although part of the state is west and north of the headwaters of the Mississippi River. Although it has been acknowledged for some time that Palaeo-Indian cultures in the east may have differed in important ways from those in the west, particularly in terms of the species hunted and hence in basic subsistence and related adaptive patterns, the Mississippi River and the Ontario-Manitoba border were arbitrarily selected because they conveniently divide the continent and not because they can be interpreted as the boundaries of two Palaeo-Indian culture areas.

The references are arranged alphabetically and by year of publication under each author. Each reference is numbered and the bibliography is followed by three cross-referenced indexes: a geographical index by province and state, an index of selected topics, and an index of selected sites and localities.

Every effort has been made to check the accuracy of each reference by referring back to the original publication. Where this was not possible it was necessary to rely on other bibliographic sources such as, for example, the library catalogue of the Peabody Museum of Archaeology and Ethnology.

Since the bibliography may be revised at some future date, I would appreciate receiving information on publications which may have been omitted or cited incorrectly as well as any suggestions for improvement.

I would like to thank Miss Nancy Jex for her work in checking the accuracy of some of the references in an earlier version of this bibliography, and Miss Peta Daniels, for the care she took in typing both manuscripts.

PLS
Toronto, November, 1973

Bibliography

Anonymous

1. N.D. "Stone relics of oldest Americans? Findings of two neatly-chipped pointed bits of stone in Virginia may prove Folsom culture of southwest became country-wide". *The Literary Digest*, p. 22.

2. 1855 "A wonderful specimen of credulous ignorance; —Fossil man and woman". *American Journal of Science and Arts*, Second Series, Vol. *XIX*, No. 57, p. 448.

3. 1878 "Discovery of a mastodon associated with human remains". *American Antiquarian*, Vol. 1, pp. 54-55.

4. 1881 "The Palaeolithic implements of the valley of the Delaware". Cambridge. Also, *Windsor Collection, Paper* No. 11, Vol. *III*.

5. 1882 Report on *The Paleolithic implements of the valley of the Delaware* by Charles C. Abbott, H.W. Haynes et al, 1881. In, *American Journal of Science and Arts*, Third Series, Vol. *XXIII*, (Whole Number *CXXIII*), No. 134, pp. 242-243.

6. 1888 "Interglacial man in Ohio". In, "Popular Miscellany," *Popular Science Monthly*, Vol. 34, p. 279.

7. 1889a Report on "Mastadon or Elephas with fragments of charcoal at Attica, Wyoming Co., N.Y.", by J.M. Clarke. In, *American Journal of Science*, Third Series, Vol. *XXXVIII* (Whole Number *CXXXVIII*), No. 225, p. 249.

8. 1889b Report on "The Ice Age in North America, and its bearings on the antiquity of man", by G. Frederick Wright, D.D. In, *American Journal of Science*, Third Series, Vol. *XXXVIII* (Whole Number *CXXXVIII*), No. 227, pp. 412-413.

9. 1890a "Interglacial man in Ohio". *Bulletin, U.S. Geological Survey*, No. 58, pp. 105-108.

10. 1890b "Stone implement at New Comerstown, Ohio". *American Journal of Science*, Third Series, Vol. *XL*, (Whole Number *CXL*), No. 235, pp. 95-96.

11. 1895 "The earliest human occupants of the Atlantic watershed". *The Archaeologist*, Vol. 3, No. 9, p. 298, Official Organ of the Ohio State Archaeological and Historical Society, Columbus, Ohio.

12. 1909 "The Wadsworth Palaeolith". *Records of the Past*, Vol. 8, pp. 111-112.

13. 1913 Report on *Origin and antiquity of man.* In, *American Journal of Science*, Fourth Series, Vol. *XXXV*, (Whole Number *CLXXXV*), No. 205, p. 110.

14. 1932 "Traces of primitive man in Florida". *El Palacio*, Vol. 32, pp. 262-263.

15. 1933 "Early people of Tennessee valley". *El Palacio*, Vol. 35, pp. 119-120.

16. 1935 "Was prehistoric man in America a hunter of mastadons and mammoths". *Science*, N.S., Vol. 82, No. 2117, Supplement, p. 10.

17. 1937 "Older than Folsom man?" *El Palacio*, Vol. 42, pp. 65-66.

18. 1939 "Folsom point [found on the Adams farm near Bridgeville, Delaware]". *Archaeological Society of Delaware, Bulletin*, Vol. 3, No. 2, p. 11.

19. 1947 "Mastodon bone artifacts". *The Tennessee Archaeologist*, Vol. 3, p. 32.

20. 1960a "Fluted points from North Carolina . . . Courtesy of Summers A. Redick . . . " *Ohio Archaeologist*, Vol. 10, p. 24.

21. 1960b "Fine Ohio Fluted points from the collection of Merle R. Sharp, Kingston, Ohio". *Ohio Archaeologist*, Vol. 10, p. 39.

22. 1962a "Further test digging at the new Paleo site (No. 2)". *Chips from the Totem Pole*, Aboriginal Research Club, Detroit, Michigan, January.

23. 1962b (Reference to the DeVisscher Paleo site No. 2.) In, *Chips from the Totem Pole*, Aboriginal Research Club, Detroit, Michigan, May.

24. 1962c (Reference to the DeVisscher Paleo site No. 2.) In, *Chips from the Totem Pole*, Aboriginal Research Club, Detroit, Michigan, November.

25. 1970 "Mammoth and mastodon remains in Orange County, New York". *The Chesopiean*, Vol. 8, No. 1, p. 9.

26. 1973a "Five lanceolate points from the central states region". *Central States Archaeological Journal*, Vol. 20, No. 1, p. 45.

27. 1973b (Report on the Timlin Site near Cobleskill, New York.) In, "Science News of the Week", *Science News*, Vol. 103, No. 21, p. 337.

Abbott, Charles C.

28. 1870 "Aboriginal relic from Trenton, New Jersey". *American Naturalist*, Vol. 4, p. 380.

29. 1872 "The Stone Age in New Jersey". *American Naturalist*, Vol. 6, No. 3, Salem, Massachusetts, pp. 144-160, 199-229. Johnson Reprint Corporation, New York and London.

30. 1873 "Occurrence of implements in the river drift at Trenton, New Jersey". *American Naturalist*, Vol. 7, No. 4, Salem, Massachusetts, pp. 204-209. Johnson Reprint Corporation, New York and London.

31. 1876a "The Stone Age in New Jersey". *Annual Report of the Board of Regents of the Smithsonian Institution for 1875*, Washington, pp. 246-380.

32. 1876b "The Stone Age in New Jersey". Trenton, New Jersey. Reprinted from, *Smithsonian Institution, Annual Report, 1875*, pp. 246-380.

33. 1877 "On the discovery of supposed Paleolithic implements in the glacial drift in the valley of the Delaware near Trenton, N.J.". *Tenth Annual Report of the Trustees of the Peabody Museum of American Archaeology and Ethnology*, Vol. 2, No. 1, pp. 30-43.

34. 1878 "Second report on the Paleolithic implements from the glacial drift, in the valley of the Delaware River, near Trenton, New Jersey". *Eleventh Annual Report of the Trustees of the Peabody Museum of Archaeology and Ethnology*, Vol. 2, No. 2, pp. 225-257.

35. 1880 "Abstract of a paper upon the traces of a people once occupying the valley of the Delaware River, supposed to have preceded the later so-called Indians". *Report of the Operation of the Numismatic and Antiquarian Society of Philadelphia for 1878-1879*.

36. 1881 *Primitive industry or illustrations of the handiwork in stone, bone and clay, of the native races of the northern Atlantic seaboard of America*. George A. Bates, Salem, Massachusetts, 560 pp.

37. 1882 "The first American". *Our Continent*, Vol. 2, No. 15, Our Continent Publishing Company, Philadelphia, pp. 469-471.

38. 1883a "Paleolithic implements from valley of Delaware River". *Congres International des Americanistes*, 5 session, Copenhagen, pp. 283-284.

39. 1883b "An historical sketch of the discoveries of Paleolithic implements in the valley of the Delaware River". *Boston Society of Natural History*, Proceedings, Vol. 21, pp. 124-132.

40. 1888 "On the antiquity of man in the valley of the Delaware". *Boston Society of Natural History*, Proceedings, vol. 23, pp. 424-426.

41. 1889a "The descendents of Palaeolithic man in America". *Popular Science Monthly*, Vol. 36, Whole No. 212, No. 2, pp. 145-153.

42. 1889b "Evidences of the antiquity of man in eastern North America". *American Association for the Advancement of Science*, Proceedings, Vol. 37, pp. 293-315.

43. 1890 "Water-worn implements from the Delaware River". *Boston Society of Natural History, Proceedings*, Vol. 24, pp. 157-158. Same in, *Paleolithic Man in Eastern and Central North America*, Part III, Cambridge, Massachusetts, 1889.

44. 1893 "Are there relics of man in the Trenton gravels?" *The Archaeologist*, Vol. 1, pp. 81-82.

45. 1904 "On the occurrence of artefacts beneath a deposit of clay". *Proceedings of the American Philosophical Society*, Vol. 43, No. 176, pp. 161-162.

Abbott, Charles C., H.W. Haynes, G.F. Wright, L. Carr, M.E. Wadsworth, and F.W. Putnam
46. 1881 "The Paleolithic implements of the valley of the Delaware". Proceedings of the Boston Society of Natural History, January 19, 1881.

Adams, J. J.
47. 1960 "A fluted point from Cabell County, W. Va.". *The West Virginia Archeologist*, No. 12, pp. 24-25.

Adams, Robert McCormick
48. 1940 "Diagnostic flint points". *American Antiquity*, "Facts and Comments," Vol. 6, No. 1, pp. 72-75.

49. 1941 "Mastodon bones from middle Mississippi refuse pits". Abstract, *Society for American Archaeology Notebook*, Vol. 2, p. 25.

Aeh, Gary R.
50. 1969 "Atheno County fluted point". *Ohio Archaeologist*, Vol. 19, No. 3, p. 83.

Agogino, George Allen
51. 1962a "A forty year look at the Paleo-Indian picture in North America". *Tennessee Archaeologist*, Vol. 18, No. 2, pp. 70-74.

52. 1962b Comments on "The Paleo-Indian tradition in eastern North America", by Ronald J. Mason. In, *Current Anthropology*, Vol. 3, No. 3, Chicago, pp. 246-247.

Allen, John W.
53. 1957 "A tool shed one million years old". *Central States Archeological Journal*, Vol. 3, pp. 97-98.

Anderson, Albert J.

54. 1967 " 'Cody knives' from Tottenville Page Avenue, Site *II*, Staten Island, New York". *The Chesopiean*, Vol. 5, No. 1, pp. 1-3.

Andrews, Edmund

55. 1875 "Dr. Koch and the Missouri mastadon". *American Journal of Science and Arts*, Third Series, Vol. *X*, (Whole Number *CX*), No. 55, pp. 32-34.

Antevs, Ernst

56. 1937 "The age of the 'Minnestoa Man' ". *Carnegie Institution of Washington, Year Book*, No. 36, pp. 335-338.

57. 1938 "Was 'Minnesota girl' buried in a gully?" *Journal of Geology*, Vol. 46, No. 3, Part *I*, pp. 293-295.

Arthurs, David

58. 1973 "Speculations on the antiquity of man in southern Ontario". *Arch Notes, Newsletter of the Ontario Archaeological Society* (Inc.), No. 4, pp. 5-10.

Babbitt, F. E.

59. 1883 "Vestiges of glacial man in Minnesota". *American Association for the Advancement of Science*, Vol. 32, pp. 385-390.

60. 1884a "Exhibition and description of some Palaeolithic quartz implements from central Minnesota". *Proceedings of the American Association for the Advancement of Science*, Vol. 33, pp. 593-599.

61. 1884b "Vestiges of glacial man in Minnesota". *American Naturalist*, Vol. 18, pp. 594-605 and 697-708.

Babbitt, Franc C.

62. 1890 "Points concerning the Little Falls quartzes". *Proceedings of the American Association for the Advancement of Science*, Vol. 38, 1889, pp. 333-339.

Baby, Raymond S., and Martha A. Potter

63. 1965 "Four fluted points from Summit County, Ohio". *Ohio Archaeologist*, Vol. 15, No. 2, pp. 64-65.

Baggerly, Carmen

64. 1954 "Waterworn and glaciated stone tools from the Thumb District of Michigan". *American Antiquity*, Vol. 20, No. 2, pp. 171-173.

65. 1956 "Artifacts of Lower Paleolithic and Eolithic pattern from drift of the Wisconsin glaciation, Cary substage, in eastern Michigan". *New World Antiquity*, Vol. 3, pp. 3-7.

Bailey, John H.

66. 1940 "A stratified rock shelter in Vermont". *Proceedings of the Vermont Historical Society,* Vol. 8, No. 1, Battleboro, pp. 3-30.

Bates, George A.

67. 1881 Report on *Primitive industry, or illustrations of the handiwork in stone, bone and clay of the native races of the northern Atlantic seaboard of America,* by Charles C. Abbott, M.D. In *American Journal of Science and Arts,* Third Series, Vol. *XXII,* (Whole Number *CXXII*), No. 131, pp. 401-402.

Beardsley, R.K., Preston Holder, Alex D. Krieger, Betty J. Meggers, John B. Rinaldo, and Paul Kutsche

68. 1956 "Functional and evolutionary implications of community patterning". In, *Seminars in Archaeology: 1955,* Robert Wauchope (Editor). *Society for American Archaeology, Memoir* No. 11, pp. 130-157.

Beauchamp, William M.

69. 1897 "Aboriginal chipped stone implements of New York". *New York State Museum, Bulletin,* Vol. 4, No. 16, 84 pp.

Behrens, Carl

70. 1971 "The search for new world man". *Science News,* Vol. 99, No. 6, pp. 98-100.

Bell, Robert E.

71. 1958 'Guide to identification of certain American Indian projectile points". *Oklahoma Anthropological Society, Special Bulletin,* No. 1.

Bennett, John W.

72. 1944 "Archaeological horizons in the southern Illinois region". *American Antiquity,* Vol. 10, pp. 12-22.

73. 1945 *Archaeological explorations in Jo Daviess County, Illinois.* University of Chicago Press, 238 pp.

74. 1952 "The prehistory of the northern Mississippi Valley". In, *Archeology of eastern United States,* James B. Griffin (Editor), The University of Chicago Press, Chicago, pp. 108-123.

Bennett, John W., and Moreau Maxwell

75. 1942 "Archaeological horizons in southern Illinois". Abstract, *Transactions of the Illinois State Academy of Science,* Vol. 35, No. 2, Springfield, p. 50.

Benthall, Joseph L.

76. 1973 "Test excavations at the Williamson Site Dinwiddie County, Virginia". Abstract, *Eastern States Archeological Federation, Bulletin* No. 32, pp. 11-12.

Berlin, A. F.
77. 1878 "Palaeolithic implements found at Reading, Pennsylvania". *American Antiquarian*, Vol. 1, pp. 10-12.

78. 1888 "Paleolithics in Pennsylvania". *American Antiquarian*, Vol. 10, pp. 250-251.

Berry, Edward W.
79. 1917 "The fossil plants from Vero, Florida". *Florida Geological Survey, Ninth Annual Report*, pp. 19-33. Also in, *Journal of Geology*, Vol. 25, No. 6, pp. 661-666.

Berthoud, C. E.
80. 1866 "Description of the Hot Springs of Soda Creek." *Proceedings of the Academy of Natural Science of Philadelphia*, Vol. 18, pp. 342-345.

Binkley S. H.
81. 1892 "Palaeolithic relics". *American Antiquarian*, Vol. 14, pp. 350-351.

Bird, Junius B.
82. 1938 "Artifacts in Canadian river terraces". *Science*, N.S., Vol. 89, No. 2311, pp. 340-341.

Black, M. J., and C. E. Eyman
83. 1963 "The Union Lake skull, a possible early Indian find in Michigan". *American Antiquity*, Vol. 29, No. 1, pp. 39-48.

Boren, Mary Lisy
84. 1971 "The marvelous monster". *Echoes,* The Ohio Historical Society, Vol. 10, No. 5, p. 1.

Borns, Harold W., Jr.
85. 1966 "The Geography of Paleo-Indian Occupation in Nova Scotia". *Tirage a part de Quaternaria, VIII,* Roma.

86. 1973 "Possible Paleo-Indian migration routes in the northeast: A geological approach". *Massachusetts Archaeological Society, Bulletin,* Vol. 34, Nos. 1-2, pp. 13-15.

Bottoms, Edward
87. 1966 "The Richmond Site: A Paleo-Indian locality in Chesterfield County, Virginia". *The Chesopean*, Vol. 4, No. 2, pp. 40-50.

88. 1969a "Survey of North Carolina Paleo-Indian projectile points, report number 1, points 1-32". *The Chesopean*, Vol. 7, No. 1, pp. 22-32.

89. 1969b "Survey of North Carolina Paleo-Indian projectile points, report number 2: points 33-52". *The Chesopean*, Vol. 7, No. 3, pp. 63-69.

90. 1969c "Notes on the geology, Pleistocene paleontology, and archaeology of Saltville, Virginia". *The Chesopiean*, Vol. 7, Nos. 4-5, pp. 80-89.

91. 1970a "Survey of North Carolina Paleo-Indian projectile points: report no. 3: points 53-67". *The Chesopiean*, Vol. 8, No. 1, pp. 14-20.

92. 1970b "Survey of North Carolina Paleo-Indian projectile points, report no. 4, points 68-94". *The Chesopiean, Vol. 8, No. 4, pp. 91-98.*

Bottoms, Edward, and Floyd Painter

93. 1965 "Facial grinding on Paleo-Indian projectile points". *The Chesopiean*, Vol. 3, No. 4, pp. 95-98.

Bowman, Mary L.

94. 1973 "A Bibliography of Kentucky Archaeology". *Kentucky Archaeological Association, Bulletin*, No. 2, 63 pp.

Boyle, David

95. 1906 "Notes on some specimens. Flints". *18th Annual Archaeological Report of Ontario 1905*, pp. 10-12.

Brain, Jeffrey P.

96. 1970 "Early Archaic in the lower Mississippi alluvial valley". *American Antiquity*, "Facts and Comments", Vol. 35, No. 1, pp. 104-105.

Brennan, Louis A.

97. 1962 "Paleo and Archaic: A realignment". *Eastern States Archeological Federation Bulletin* No. 21, pp. 10-11.

98. 1963 "A short evaluation of the current state of knowledge of New York prehistory stated in terms of the problems raised by it". *New York State Archeological Association, The Bulletin*, No. 28, pp. 6-15.

99. 1965 "Supplementary comment" to "Fluted point discovered in Orange County cave", by Robert E. Funk, George Walters, and William F. Ehlers. In, *New York State Archeological Association, The Bulletin*, No. 34, pp. 4-6.

100. 1966a "The earliest occupants—Paleo-Indian hunters: a review". *New York State Archeological Association, The Bulletin*, No. 36, pp. 2-4.

101. 1966b "The archaeology of New York state: A summary review". *New York State Archeological Association, The Bulletin*, No. 36, pp. 14-17.

102. 1970 *American dawn: A new model of American prehistory.* The Macmillan Company, Collier-Macmillan Limited, London.

103. 1972 "The implications of two recent radiocarbon dates from Montrose Point on the lower Hudson River". *Pennsylvania Archaeologist*, Vol. 42, Nos. 1-2, pp. 1-14.

Brenning, Edward
104. 1961 "A Yuma-type point from Minnesota". *Minnesota Archaeologist*, Vol. 23, No. 2, p. 38.

Brew, John Otis
105. 1943 "A selected bibliography of American Indian archaeology east of the Rocky Mountains". *Excavators' Club, Papers*, Vol. 2, No. 1, 90 pp.

Brewer, Jesse
106. 1965 "Suwanee point finds in Florida". *Massachusetts Archaeological Society, Bulletin*, Vol. 26, No. 2, pp. 17-19.

Brock, Oscar W.
107. 1967 "Lameller blades of possible Paleo Indian provenience from Alabama". *Journal of Alabama Archaeology*, Vol. 13, No. 2, pp. 99-114.

Brooks, H.B.
108. 1973 "The finding of the Cole Cumberland". *Central States Archaeological Journal*, Vol. 20, No. 1, pp. 40-43.

Brown, Calvin, S.
109. 1926 *Archaeology of Mississippi*. Mississippi Geological Survey, University, Missouri.

Brown, James, and Charles Cleland
110. 1968 "The late glacial and early postglacial faunal resources in midwestern biomes newly opened to human adaptation". In, *The Quaternary of Illinois*, Robert E. Bergstrom (Editor), *University of Illinois, College of Agriculture, Special Publication*, No. 14, Urbana, Illinois, pp. 114-122.

Brown, Virgil
111. 1963 "How I came to get a Folsom". *Ohio Archaeologist*, Vol. XIII, pp. 32-33.

Browner, Thomas E.
112. 1971 "Contributions of amateurs to the discovery of Paleo-Indian sites in North America". *Central States Archaeological Journal*, Vol. 18, No. 4, pp. 152-161.

Broyles, Bettye J.
113. 1958 "Russell Cave in Northern Alabama". *Tennessee Archaeological Society, Miscellaneous Paper* 4, 35 pp.

114. 1967 "Henry Kelly collection". *West Virginia Archeological Society, Newsletter*, Vol. 9, No. 2, p. 2.

Brunett, Fel V.
115. 1966 "An archaeological survey of the Manistee River basin: Sharon,

Michigan to Sherman, Michigan". *Michigan Archaeologist*, Vol. 12, No. 4, pp. 169-182.

Bryan, Alan L.
116. 1968 "Some problems and hypotheses relative to early entry of man into America". *Anthropologica*, N.S., Vol. X, pp. 157-177.

Bryan, Kirk
117. 1935 "Minnesota man—A discussion of the site". *Science*, N.S., Vol. 82, pp. 170-171.

118. 1937 "Ancient man in America". *Geographical Review*, Vol. 27, pp. 507-509.

119. 1941 "Geologic antiquity of man in America". *Science*, N.S., Vol. 93, pp. 505-514.

Bryan, Kirk, and Paul MacClintock
120. 1938 "What is implied by 'disturbance' at the site of Minnesota man". *Journal of Geology*, Vol. 46, No. 3, Part I, pp. 279-292.

Bryan, Kirk, Henry Retzek, and Franklin T. McCann
121. 1938 "Discovery of Sauk Valley man of Minnesota, with an account of the geology". *Texas Archaeological and Paleontological Society, Bulletin*, Vol. 10, pp. 114-135.

Bullen, Ripley P.
122. 1946 Review of *Archaeology of New Jersey, Volume I* by Dorothy Cross. In, *Massachusetts Archaeological Society, Bulletin*, Vol. 8, No. 1, pp. 8-10.

123. 1951 "Culture growth and change in eastern Massachusetts". *Massachusetts Archaeological Society, Bulletin*, Vol. 13, pp. 8-10.

124. 1958 "The Bolen Bluff Site on Paynes Prairie, Florida". *Florida State Museum, Social Sciences, Contributions*, No. 4.

125. 1962 "Suwannee points in the Simpson collection". *Florida Anthropologist*, Vol. 15, No. 3, pp. 83-88.

126. 1967 "A Florida Folsom (?) point". *Florida Anthropologist*, Vol. 20, Nos. 1-2, p. 2.

127. 1968 *A guide to the identification of Florida projectile points*. Florida State Museum, Gainesville, 50 pp.

128. 1969 "A Clovis fluted point from the Sante Fe River, Florida". *Florida Anthropologist*, Vol. 22, Nos. 1-4, pp. 36-37.

Bullen, Ripley P., and Laurence E. Beilman
129. 1973 "The Nalcrest Site, Lake Weohyakapka, Florida". *Florida Anthropologist*, Vol. 26, No. 1, pp. 1-22.

Bullen, Ripley P., S. David Webb, and Benjamin I. Waller
130. 1970 "A worked mammoth bone from Florida". *American Antiquity*, Vol. 35, No. 2, pp. 203-205.

Bullen, Ripley P., and Marjorie H. Wing
131. 1968 "A scraper with graver spurs from Florida". *Florida Anthropologist*, Vol. 21, Nos. 2-3, pp. 94-95.

Burbage, Beverly S.
132. 1962 "Paleo-Indian points and uniface material from the Clinch River valley". *Tennessee Archaeologist*, Vol. 18, No. 1, pp. 46-51.

Burns, Alice M.
133. 1967 "Pebble tool traits on other then pebbles". *Anthropological Journal of Canada*, Vol. 5, No. 2, pp. 16-18.

Burns, Alice M., A.G. Long, Jr., and Daniel W. Josselyn
134. 1968 "Lively complex tools on other then pebbles". *Journal of Alabama Archaeology*, Vol. 14, No. 2, pp. 51-61.

Bushnell, David I., Jr.
135. 1935 "The Manahoac tribes in Virginia, 1608". *Smithsonian Institution, Miscellaneous Collections*, Vol. 95, 56 pp.

136. 1941 "Trailing Early Man in Virginia". *Explorations and Field-Work of the Smithsonian Institution in 1940, Smithsonian Institution, Publication* No. 3631, Washington, pp. 75-78.

Butzer, Karl W.
137. 1971 *Environment and archaeology: an ecological approach to prehistory*. Aldine-Atherton, Chicago and New York, 2nd Edition, 703 pp.

Byers, Douglas S.
138. 1942 "Fluted points from Wisconsin". *American Antiquity*, Vol. 7, No. 4, p. 400.

139. 1954 "Bull Brook—A fluted point site in Ipswich, Massachusetts". *American Antiquity*, Vol. 19, No. 4, pp. 343-351.

140. 1955 "Additional information on the Bullbrook Site, Massachusetts". *American Antiquity*, Vol. 20, No. 3, pp. 274-276.

141. 1956 "Ipswich B.C.". *Essex Institute Historical Collections*, Essex.

142. 1957 "Ipswich, B.C." *Massachusetts Archaeological Society*, Bulletin, Vol. 18, No. 3, pp. 49-55.

143. 1959a "Radiocarbon dates for the Bull Brook Site, Massachusetts". *American Antiquity*, Vol. 24, No. 4, Part I, pp. 427-429.

144. 1959b "Two sites in southern New England". *Massachusetts Archaeological Society, Bulletin*, Vol. 20, No. 1, pp. 1-7.

145. 1959c "Radiocarbon dates from Bull Brook". *Massachusetts Archaeological Society, Bulletin*, Vol. 20, No. 3, p. 33.

146. 1962 Comments on "The Paleo-Indian tradition in eastern North America", by Ronald J. Mason. In, *Current Anthropology*, Vol. 3, No. 3, Chicago, pp. 247-250.

147. 1966 "The Debert archaeological project: the position of Debert with respect to the Paleo-Indian tradition". *Tirage a part de Quaternaria*, VIII, Roma.

148. 1969 "Debert and delirium: Early Man in Nova Scotia". *Eastern States Archeological Federation, Bulletin*, Nos. 26 and 27, p. 11.

Byers, Douglas S. and W.S. Hadlock
149. 1955 "Carbon-14 dates from Ellsworth Falls, Maine". *Science*, Vol. 121, pp. 735-736.

Cain, L.K.
150. 1969 "Some probable late Paleo-Indian early Archaic projectile points from east central Minnesota". *Minnesota Archaeologist*, Vol. 30, No. 2, pp. 45-48.

Caine, Christy A.H.
151. 1968 "Big-game hunting artifacts in Minnesota". *Plains Anthropologist*, Vol. 13, No. 40, pp. 87-89.

Caldwell, Joseph R.
152. 1952 "The archeology of eastern Georgia and South Carolina". In, *Archeology of eastern United States*, James B. Griffin (Editor), The University of Chicago Press, Chicago, pp. 312-321.

153. 1954 "The old quartz industry of Piedmont Georgia and South Carolina". *Southern Indian Studies VI*, pp. 37-39.

154. 1958 "Trend and tradition in the prehistory of the eastern United States". *Illinois State Museum Scientific Papers*, Vol. X, and *American Anthropological Association*, Memoir 88, 88 pp.

Cambron, James W.
155. 1955 "Preliminary report on the stone pipe site in north Alabama". *The Tennessee Archaeologist*, Vol. 11, No. 4, pp. 54-62.

156.   1956   "The Pine Tree Site—A Paleo-Indian habitation locality". *The Tennessee Archaeologist*, Vol. 12, No. 2, pp. 1-10.

157.   1957   "Some early projectile point types from the Tennessee Valley, Parts I-V". *Journal of Alabama Archaeology*, Vol. 3, No. 2, pp. 17-19; Vol. 4, No. 1, pp. 17-19; Vol. 4, No. 2, pp. 10-12; Vol. 5, No. 1, pp. 11-12; Vol. 5, No. 3, pp. 73-74. Title varies.

158.   1958   "Paleo points from the Pine Tree Site". *The Tennessee Archaeologist*, Vol. 14, No. 2, pp. 80-84.

159.   1963   "Fluted points found in situ". *Journal of Alabama Archaeology*, Vol. 5, No. 3, pp. 75-76.

Cambron, James W., and David C. Hulse
160.   1960   "An excavation at the Quad Site". *Tennessee Archaeologist*, Vol. 16, No. 1, pp. 14-26.

Cambron, James W., and Spencer A. Waters
161.   1959   "Flint Creek rockshelter (Part 1)". *Tennessee Archaeologist*, Vol. 15, No. 2, pp. 72-87.

Carr, L.
162.   1881   "Statement relating to the finding of an implement in the gravel". In, *The Palaeolithic implements of the valley of the Delaware*, by Charles C. Abbott. *Windsor Collection, Paper* No. 11, Vol. III, pp. 145-146.

Carskadden, Jeff
163.   1966   "Palaeo-Indian points from Muskingum County". *Ohio Archaeologist*, Vol. 16, No. 1, pp. 4-5.

Carter, George F.
164.   1956   "Artifacts from the glacial gravels". *Ohio Archaeologist*, Vol. 6, pp. 82-84.

165.   1958   "Sea level—time—and coastal archeology in the east". *Eastern States Archeological Federation, Bulletin*, No. 17, pp. 14-15.

166.   1966   "On pebble tools and their relatives in North America". *Anthropological Journal of Canada*, Vol. 4, No. 4, pp. 10-19.

167.   1972   "Early Man in America". *Anthropological Journal of Canada*, Vol. 10, No. 3, pp. 2-9.

Case, Ermine, et al
168.   1934   "Discovery of *Elephas primigenius americanus* in the bed of glacial Lake Mogodore; in Cass County, Michigan". *Papers of the Michigan Academy of Science, Arts, and Letters*, Vol. 20, pp. 449-454.

Cassell, Raymond, K.
169. 1941 "A postulated corridor of Folsom migration". *Papers of the Michigan Academy of Science, Arts, and Letters*, Vol. 26, pp. 451-457.

Casson, Stanley
170. 1939 *The discovery of man.* Harper and Brothers, New York, 339 pp.

Chamberlain, Rollin T.
171. 1917a "Interpretation of the formations containing human bones at Vero, Florida". *Journal of Geology*, Vol. 25, No. 1, pp. 25-39.

172. 1917b "Further studies at Vero, Florida". *Journal of Geology*, Vol. 25, No. 7, pp. 667-683.

Chard, Chester S.
173. 1962 Comments on "The Paleo-Indian tradition in eastern North America", by Ronald J. Mason. In, *Current Anthropology*, Vol. 3, No. 3, Chicago, p. 250.

Clarke, John Mason
174. 1887 "Mastadon or Elephas with fragments of Charcoal at Attica, Wyoming Co., N.Y.". *The Report for 1887 of the State Museum of New York.*

175. 1888 "Report on bones of mastodon or Elephas, found in association with human relics in the village of Attica". Pamphlet.

176. 1903 "Mastodons of New York, a list of discoveries of their remains 1705-1902". *New York State Museum, Bulletin* 69, pp. 921-933.

Claypole, E.W.
177. 1896 "Human relics in the drift of Ohio". *American Geologist*, Vol. 18, pp. 302-314.

Cleland, Charles Edward
178. 1965 "Barren ground caribou (*Rangifer arcticus*) from an Early Man site in southeastern Michigan". *American Antiquity*, Vol. 30, No. 3, pp. 350-351.

179. 1966 "The prehistoric animal ecology and ethnozoology of the upper Great Lakes region". *Anthropological Papers, Museum of Anthropology*, University of Michigan, No. 29, 294 pp.

Coe, Joffre L.
180. 1949 "The oldest culture in North Carolina?" *Southern Indian Studies*, Vol. 1, No. 1, Chapel Hill, p. 15.

181. 1952 "The cultural sequence of the Carolina Piedmont". In, *Archeology of the eastern United States*, James B. Griffin (Editor). The University of Chicago Press, Chicago, pp. 301-311.

182. 1964 "The formative cultures of the Carolina Piedmont". *Transactions of the American Philosophical Society*, N.S., Vol. 54, Part 5, Philadelphia.

Connally, G. Gordon
183. 1970 "Discussion, caribou and Paleo-Indian in New York State: A presumed association". *American Journal of Science*, Vol. 269, No. 3, pp. 314-315.

Connery, J.H.
184. 1932 "Recent find of mammoth remains in the quaternary of Florida, together with arrowhead". *Science*, N.S., Vol. 75, No. 1950, p. 516.

Cooke, C. Wythe
185. 1926 "Fossil man and Pleistocene vertebrates in Florida". *American Journal of Science*, Fifth Series, Vol. XII, (Whole Number *CCXII*), No. 71, pp. 441-452.

186. 1928 "The stratigraphy and age of the Pleistocene deposits in Florida from which human bones have been reported". *Washington Academy of Science, Journal*, Vol. 18, No. 15, pp. 414-421.

Cooke, C. Wythe, and Stuart Mossom
187. 1929 "Geology of Florida". *Florida Geological Survey, Twentieth Annual Report*, pp. 218-226.

Cooper, Peter P.
188. 1967 "Early points on the Upper Yadkin, N.C.". *Anthropological Journal of Canada*, Vol. 5, No. 1, p. 11.

189. 1970 "Piedmont archaeological survey". *Anthropological Journal of Canada*, Vol. 8, No. 1, pp. 24-25.

190. 1972 "The southeastern archaeological area re-defined". *Archeological Society of Virginia, Quarterly Bulletin*, Vol. 26, No. 3, pp. 136-144.

Cotter, John L. (Assembler)
191. 1962 "Massachusetts". *American Antiquity*, "News and Notes", Vol. 27, No. 3, p. 456.

192. 1962 Comments on "The Paleo-Indian tradition in eastern North America", by Ronald J. Mason. In, *Current Anthropology*, Vol. 3, No. 3, Chicago, pp. 250-252.

Crane, H.R., and James B. Griffin
193. 1958 "University of Michigan radiocarbon dates *II*". *Science*, Vol. 127 No. 3306, pp. 1098-1105.

Cresson, Hilborne Thomson

194. 1890 "Early Man in the Delaware Valley". *Proceedings of the Boston Society of Natural History*, Vol. 24, pp. 141-150.

195. 1892 "Paleolithic man in the southern portion of the Delaware Valley". *Science*, 2nd Series, Vol. 20, p. 304.

Cross, Dorothy

196. 1941 *Archeology of New Jersey*, Vol. 1. Trenton, New Jersey.

197. 1943 "The effect of the Abbott Farm on eastern chronology". *Proceedings of the American Philosophical Society*, Vol. 86, Philadelphia, pp. 315-319.

198. 1956 *Archaeology of New Jersey, Volume 2: The Abbott Farm.* The Archaeological Society of New Jersey and the New Jersey State Museum Trenton.

Crozier, Archibald

199. 1939 "Delaware Folsom points". *Archaeological Society of Delaware, Bulletin* Vol. 3, No. 1, Wilmington, pp. 8-10.

Dana, James D.

200. 1875a "On Dr. Koch's evidence with regard to the contemporaneity of man and the mastodon in Missouri". *American Journal of Science and Arts,* Third Series, Vol. IX, (Whole Number *CIX*), No. 53, pp. 335-346, 398.

201. 1875b "On southern New England during the melting of the great glacier: No. *III*". *American Journal of Science and Arts,* Third Series, Vol. *X*, (Whole Number *CX*), No. 59, pp. 353-357.

Davis, E.L.

202. 1969 "The western lithic co-tradition". In, *The western lithic co-tradition,* by E.L. Davis, C.W. Brott and D.L. Weide. *San Diego Museum Papers,* No. 6, pp. 11-78.

Davis, Watson

203. 1932 "Dr. Jenks finds maiden of Ice Age". *El Palacio*, Vol. 33, pp. 239-240.

De Jarnette, David L.

204. 1952 "Alabama Archeology: A Summary". In, *Archeology of Eastern United States,* James B. Griffin (Editor). The University of Chicago Press, Chicago, pp. 272-284.

205. 1962 "Stanfield-Worley shelter excavation—preliminary report". *Eastern States Archeological Federation Bulletin* No. 21, p. 13.

206. 1964 "Fluted projectile points in a stratified site in Marshall County, Alabama". *Eastern States Archeological Federation, Bulletin* No. 23, pp. 13-14.

207. 1967 "Alabama pebble tools: The Lively complex". *Eastern States Archeological Federation, Bulletin* No. 26, pp. 11-12.

DeJarnette, David L., E.B. Kurjack, and J.W. Cambron

208. 1962 "Stanfield-Worley bluff shelter excavations". *Journal of Alabama Archaeology*, Vol. 8, Nos. 1 and 2.

Dekin, Albert A.

209. 1966 "A fluted point from Grand Traverse County". *Michigan Archaeologist*, Vol. 12, No. 1, pp. 35-36.

Deplante, Don

210. 1953 "Manitoulin relics 70 centuries old". *The Totem Pole*, Vol. 32, No. 4, pp. 1-4.

Deuel, Thorne

211. 1958 "American Indian ways of life: An interpretation of the archaeology of Illinois and adjoining areas". *Illinois State Museum, Story of Illinois Series*, No. 9, Springfield, Illinois, 76 pp.

DeVisscher, Jerry

212. 1963 "Surface finds on various parts of the Holcombe Site beach". *The Totem Pole*, Vol. 46, No. 5, May, Aboriginal Research Club, Detroit, Michigan, pp. 37-38.

DeVisscher, Jerry, and Edward J. Wahla

213. 1964 "Paleo-*II*-W: A minor Paleo-Indian occupation site in Macomb County, Michigan". *Michigan Archaeologist*, Vol. 10, No. 1, pp. 5-10.

DeVisscher, Jerry, and Edward J. Wahla, with chippage analysis by James E. Fitting

214. 1970 "Additional Paleo-Indian campsites adjacent to the Holcombe Site". *The Michigan Archaeologist*, Vol. 16, No. 1, pp. 1-23.

Dickeson, M.W.

215. 1846 "Fossils from Natchez, Mississippi". *Proceedings of the Academy of Natural Science of Philadelphia*, Vol. 3, No. 5, pp. 106-107.

Dickson, James A.

216. 1967 "A rock crystal fluted point from the Cumberland Valley, Pennsylvania". *Pennsylvania Archaeologist*, Vol. 37, Nos. 1-2, pp. 1-4.

Dietz, Eugene F.

217. 1956 "Early Man in Wisconsin and subsoil archaeology". *Wisconsin Archeologist*, Vol. 37, No. 2, pp. 33-45.

Dilatush, Donald

218.   1960   "Problem tools". *Archeological Society of New Jersey, Bulletin*, No. 17, p. 11.

Dilks, Margaret Day, and George M. Reynolds

219.   1962   "A survey of fluted points found in the Susquehanna Basin: Report no. 3 the upper Chesapeake Bay area." *Pennsylvania Archaeologist*, Vol. 32, No. 2, pp. 56-58.

220.   1965   "A preliminary report on 'A survey of fluted points in Maryland' ". *Archaeological Society of Maryland, Journal*, Vol. 1, No. 1, 3 pp.

Dorwin, John T.

221.   1966   "Fluted points and Late-Pleistocene Geochronology in Indiana". *Indiana Historical Society, Prehistory Research Series*, Vol. IV, No. III.

Dragoo, Don W.

222.   1959   "Archaic hunters of the upper Ohio Valley". *Carnegie Museum, Annals* 35, No. 10, pp. 139-246.

Dragoo, Don W. (Editor)

223.   1963   Report of an address by Olaf H. Prufer at the general meeting of the Society for Pennsylvania Archaeology. In, *Archeological Newsletter*, No. 26, Section of Man, Carnegie Museum, Pittsburgh, p. 6.

224.   1964a   (Report on Wells Creek Crater Paleo-Indian Site.) In, "News and Notes", *Archeological Newsletter*, No. 29, Section of Man, Carnegie Museum, Pittsburgh, p. 1.

Dragoo, Don W.

225.   1964b   "Investigations of two Early Man sites in the Ohio Valley drainage". *Year Book of the American Philosophical Society*, Philadelphia, pp. 488-489.

226.   1965a   "Investigations at a Paleo-Indian site in Stewart County, Tennessee". *Eastern States Archeological Federation, Bulletin* No. 24, pp. 12-13.

Dragoo, Don W. (Editor)

227.   1965b   "Early Man project". "News and Notes", *Archeological Newsletter*, No. 32, Section of Man, Carnegie Museum, Pittsburg, p. 1.

228.   1967a   "Early Man in eastern North America". *Eastern States Archeological Federation, Bulletin* No. 26, p. 11.

Dragoo, Don W. (Editor)

229.   1967b   "Field work 1967". In, "News and Notes", *Archeological Newsletter*, No. 38, Section of Man, Carnegie Museum, Pittsburgh, p. 3.

230. 1970 "Early Man project". In, "News and Notes", *Archeological Newsletter*, Nos. 45-46, Section of Man, Carnegie Museum, Pittsburgh, pp. 1-2.

Drake, D.
231. 1850 "Human remains from alluvial deposits at New Orleans". In, *A systematic treatise on the principal diseases of the interior valley of North America*, etc., Cincinnati, pp. 76-77.

Drake, R.J.
232. 1962 Comments on "The Paleo-Indian tradition in eastern North America", by Ronald J. Mason. In, *Current Anthropology*, Vol. 3, No. 3, Chicago, p. 252.

Dreimanis, A.
233. 1967 "Mastodons, their geologic age and extinction in Ontario, Canada". *Canadian Journal of Earth Sciences*, Volume 4, No. 3, pp. 663-675.

234. 1968 "Extinction of mastodons in eastern North America: : Testing a new climatic-environmental hypothesis". *The Ohio Journal of Science*, Vol. 68, No. 6, pp. 257-272.

Dressler, Frank J.
235. 1931 "More About the Richmond Mastadon; Unexpected Discoveries are Made on the Site". *Hobbies*, Vol. 12, Buffalo, pp. 38-39.

Drumm, Judith
236. 1963 "Mammoths and mastodons, ice age elephants of New York". *State Museum and Science Service, Educational Leaflet* 13, The University of the State of New York, 31 pp.

Eddy, Samuel, and Albert E Jenks
237. 1935 "A kitchen midden with bones of extinct animals in the upper lakes area". *Science*, N.S., Vol. 81, No. 2109, p. 535.

Eiseley, L.S.
238. 1945 "The mastodon and Early Man in America". *Science*, N.S., Vol. 102, pp. 108-110.

Eldridge, William and Joseph Vacaro
239. 1952 "The Bull Brook Site, Ipswich, Mass.". *Massachusetts Archaeological Society, Bulletin*, Vol. 13, pp. 39-43.

Emanuel, William H.
240. 1968 "The American 'hand axe' ". *Tennessee Archaeologist*, Vol. 24, No. 1, pp. 8-28.

Emery, K.O.
241. 1966 "Early Man may have roamed the Atlantic Shelf". *Oceanus*, Vol. 12, No. 2, Woods Hole.

Epstein, Jeremiah F.
242. 1967 "Two burin-faceted points from Coshocton County, Ohio". *Ohio Archaeologist*, Vol. 17, No. 2, pp. 62-64.

Fairbanks, Charles H.
243. 1952 "Creek and pre-Creek". In, *Archeology of eastern United States*, James B. Griffin (Editor), The University of Chicago Press, Chicago, pp. 285-300.

Fairchild, Jerry
244. 1970 "The Kralosky Site". *Michigan Archaeologist*, Vol. 16, No. 1, pp. 33-42.

Fenstermaker, Gerald B.
245. 1941 "Folsom points in early Pennsylvania collections". *Pennsylvania Archaeologist*, Vol. 11, p. 62.

Fincham, Glenval
246. 1970a "A suggested explanation for modified eastern Scottsbluff points". *Redskin*, Vol. 5, No. 4, pp. 104-107.

247. 1970b "A suggested explanation for the semi-unmodified base which sometimes occurs in the eastern Scottsbluff". *The Michigan Archaeologist*, Vol. 16, No. 1, pp. 25-31.

Fink, Paul M.
248. 1945 "Early Man in Washington County". *Tennessee Archaeologist*, Vol. 1, No. 4, pp. 6-8.

Fischel, Hans E.
249. 1941 "Supplementary data on Early Man in America". *American Antiquity*, Vol. 6, No. 4, pp. 346-348.

Fitting, James E.
250. 1963a "An early post fluted point tradition in Michigan: A distributional analysis". *The Michigan Archaeologist*, Vol. 9, No. 2, pp. 21-25.

251. 1963b "The Hi-Lo Site: A late Paleo-Indian site in western Michigan". *The Wisconsin Archeologist*, N.S., Vol. 44, No. 2, pp. 87-96.

252. 1963c "The Welti Site: A multi-component site in southeastern Michigan". *Michigan Archaeologist*, Vol. 9, No. 3, pp. 34-40.

253. 1963d "The Hi-Lo Site: A progress report". *The Coffinberry News Bulletin*, Vol. X, No. 6, June, Wright L. Coffinberry Chapter, Michigan Archaeological Society, Grand Rapids, pp. 57-58.

254. 1963e "Thickness and fluting of Paleo-Indian projectile points". *American Antiquity*, Vol. 29, No. 1, pp. 105-106.

255. 1964 "Some characteristics of projectile point bases from the Holcombe Site, Macomb County, Michigan". *Papers of the Michigan Academy of Science, Arts, and Letters*, Vol. 49, pp. 231-239.

256. 1965a "A preliminary report on a quantitative examination of Paleo-Indian projectile points in the eastern United States". *Papers of the Michigan Academy of Science, Arts, and Letters*, Vol. 50, pp. 365-371.

257. 1965b "A quantitative examination of Virginia fluted points". *American Antiquity*, Vol. 30, No. 4, pp. 484-491.

258. 1965c "Observations on Paleo-Indian adaptive and settlement patterns". *Michigan Archaeologist*, Vol. 11, Nos. 3-4, pp. 103-109.

259. 1966 "The archeology explosion in Michigan". *Eastern States Archeological Federation, Bulletin*, No. 25, p. 10.

260. 1967 "Early Man in the upper Great Lakes region". *Eastern States Archeological Federation, Bulletin*, No. 26, p. 12.

261. 1968 "Environmental potential and the post-glacial readaptation in eastern North America". *American Antiquity*, Vol. 33, No. 4, pp. 441-444.

262. 1970 *The archaeology of Michigan: A guide to the prehistory of the Great Lakes region.* The Natural History Press, Garden City, New York.

Fitting, James E., Jerry DeVisscher, and Edward J. Wahla
263. 1966 "The Paleo-Indian occupation of the Holcombe Beach". *Anthropological Papers, Museum of Anthropology, University of Michigan*, No. 27, Ann Arbor, 147 pp.

Flanders, Richard E.
264. 1971 Review of, *The archaeology of Michigan: A guide to the prehistory of the Great Lakes region*, by James E. Fitting. *The Michigan Archaeologist*, Vol. 17, No. 1, pp. 47-48.

Flaskerd, George A.
265. 1945 "Some Folsom and Yuma type points from Minnesota". *Minnesota Archaeologist*, Vol. 11, No. 2, pp. 32-33.

Flint, Richard Foster
266. 1953 Report on *Early Man in America*, by E.H. Sellards. In, *American Journal of Science*, Vol. 251, No. 9, pp. 691-692.

Flint, Richard Foster, and Edward S. Deevey, Jr. (Editors)
267. 1959 American Journal of Science Radiocarbon Supplement, Vol. 1, Yale University, New Haven, Connecticut.

268. 1960 American Journal of Science Radiocarbon Supplement, Vol. 2, Yale University, New Haven, Connecticut.

Forbis, Richard G.
269. 1962 Comments on, "The Paleo-Indian tradition in eastern North America", by Ronald J. Mason. In, *Current Anthropology*, Vol. 3, No. 3, Chicago, p. 252.

Ford, James H., and Gordon R. Willey
270. 1941 "An interpretation of the prehistory of the eastern United States". *American Anthropologist*, N.S., Vol. 43, No. 3, pp. 325-363.

Ford, Joe
271. 1968 "Early site in McLean County, Kentucky". *Central States Archaeological Journal*, Vol. 15, No. 1, pp. 12-13.

Foster, J.W.
272. 1874 *Pre-historic races of the United States of America.* Third Edition, S.C. Griggs and Company, Chicago, 415 pp.

Fowke, Gerard
273. 1896 "Stone art". *Bureau of American Ethnology, 13th Annual Report 1891-'92*, pp. 47-178.

Fowler, Jeen Hodges
274. 1970 "Beeks". *Anthropological Journal of Canada*, Vol. 8, No. 1, pp. 47-48.

Fowler, Melvin L.
275. 1954 "Some fluted projectile points from Illinois". *American Antiquity*, "Facts and Comments", Vol. 20, No. 2, pp. 170-171.

276. 1952-54 "Radiocarbon dates and Illinois archaeology". *Illinois State Archaeological Society, Journal*, N.S., Vol. 2, pp. 97-103; Vol. 4, pp. 28-32.

277. 1959 "Summary report of Modoc rock shelter 1952, 1953, 1955, 1956". *Illinois State Museum Report of Investigations* No. 8, 72 pp.

Fowler, Melvin L., and P.W. Parmalee

278. 1959 "Ecological interpretation of data on archaeological sites: The Modoc rock shelter". *Transactions of the Illinois Academy of Science,* Vol. 52, Nos. 3 and 4, pp. 109-119.

Fowler, Melvin L., and Howard D. Winters

279. 1956 "Modoc rock shelter preliminary report". *Illinois State Museum Report of Investigations* 4.

Fowler, William Smith

280. 1952 "Twin Rivers: Four culture sequence at a Rhode Island site". With "Geology of the site" by J.P. Schefer. *Massachusetts Archaeological Society Bulletin,* Vol. 14, No. 1, pp. 1-18.

281. 1953 "A proposed artifact classification". *Massachusetts Archaeological Society Bulletin,* Vol. 15, No. 1, pp. 9-20.

282. 1954a "Fluted points of New England". *Eastern States Archeological Federation, Bulletin,* Vol. 13, p. 7.

283. 1954b "Massachusetts fluted points". *Massachusetts Archaeological Society, Bulletin,* Vol. 16, No. 1, pp. 2-8.

284. 1956 "Massachusetts fluted points". In, *Preliminary classification outlines, Massachusetts Archaeological Society,* Attleboro, pp. 26-30.

285. 1961a "Movement of prehistoric peoples in the northeast". *Massachusetts Archaeological Society, Bulletin,* Vol. 22, pp. 62-65.

286. 1961b "Projectile points and their cultural significance". *Massachusetts Archaeological Society, Bulletin* Vol. 23, No. 1, pp. 5-13.

287. 1963a "Correlation of seven sites in the Narragansett Bay drainage". *Massachusetts Archaeological Society, Bulletin,* Vol. 24, Nos. 3 and 4, pp. 37-44.

288. 1963b "Classification of stone implements of the northeast". *Massachusetts Archaeological Society, Bulletin,* Vol. 25, No. 1, pp. 1-29.

289. 1964 "Contributions to the advance of New England archaeology". *Massachusetts Archaeological Society, Bulletin,* Vol. 25, Nos. 3 and 4, pp. 50-69.

290. 1968 "A case for an early Archaic in New England". *Massachusetts Archaeological Society, Bulletin,* Vol. 29, Nos. 3 and 4, pp. 53-58.

291. 1970 "Recent Boats Site early Archaic recoveries". *Massachusetts Archaeological Society, Bulletin,* Vol. 31, Nos. 3 and 4, pp. 29-30.

292. 1972 "Eden points in Massachusetts". *Massachusetts Archaeological Society, Bulletin*, Vol. 33, Nos. 3 and 4, pp. 29-31.

293. 1973a "Abodes of four aboriginal periods". *Massachusetts Archaeological Society, Bulletin*, Vol. 34, Nos. 3 and 4, pp. 15-22.

294. 1973b "Bull Brook: A Paleo complex site". *Massachusetts Archaeological Society, Bulletin*, Vol. 34, Nos. 1 and 2, pp. 1-6.

Freeman, John D.
295. 1957 "Stemmed and notched fluted points". *Tennessee Archaeologist*, Vol. 13, No. 2, pp. 87-91.

Funk, Robert E.
296. 1967 "A Paleo-Indian site in the Hudson Valley". *Eastern States Archeological Federation, Bulletin*, No. 26, pp. 9-10.

297. 1972 "Early Man in the northeast and the late-glacial environment". *Man in the Northeast*, No. 4, pp. 7-39.

Funk, Robert E., Donald W. Fisher, and Edgar M. Reilly, Jr.
298. 1970 "Caribou and Paleo-Indian in New York State: —A presumed association". *American Journal of Science*, Vol. 268, No. 2, pp. 181-186.

Funk, Robert E., and R. Arthur Johnson
299. 1964 "A probable Paleo-Indian component in Greene County, New York". *Pennsylvania Archaeologist*, Vol. 34, No. 1, pp. 43-46.

Funk, Robert E., and Frank F. Schambach
300. 1964 "Probable Plano points in New York State". *Pennsylvania Archaeologist*, Vol. 34, No. 2, pp. 90-93.

Funk, Robert E., George R. Walters, and William F. Ehlers, Jr.
301. 1965 "Fluted point discovered in Orange County cave". *New York State Archeological Association, The Bulletin*, Vol. 34, pp. 2-4.

302. 1969a "A radiocarbon date for Early Man from the Dutchess Quarry cave". *New York State Archeological Association, The Bulletin*, No. 46, pp. 19-21.

303. 1969b "The archeology of Dutchess Quarry cave, Orange County, New York". With a report on faunal remains by John E. Guilday and a report on glacial history by G. Gordon Connally. *Pennsylvania Archaeologist*, Vol. 39, Nos. 1-4, pp. 7-22.

Funk, Robert E., Thomas P. Weinman, and Paul L. Weinman
304. 1969 "The Kings Road Site: A recently discovered Paleo-Indian manifestation in Greene County, New York". *New York State Archeological Association, The Bulletin*, Number 45, pp. 1-23.

Gaenslen, George
305. 1970 "How glaciers affected the greater Milwaukee area". *Lore*, Vol. 20, No. 4, pp. 116-129.

Gagliano, Sherwood M.
306. 1963 "A survey of preceramic occupations in portions of south Louisiana and south Mississippi". *Florida Anthropologist*, Vol. XVI, No. 4, pp. 105-132.

307. 1964 "Post-Pleistocene occupations of southeastern Louisiana terrace lands". In, Proceedings of the 19th Southeastern Archaeological Conference, Moundville, Alabama, 1962. *Southeastern Archaeological Conference Bulletin*, No. 1, Cambridge, Massachusetts, pp. 18-26.

Gagliano, Sherwood M., and Hiram F. Gregory
308. 1965 "A preliminary survey of Paleo-Indian points from Louisiana". *Louisiana Studies*, Vol. 4, No. 1, pp. 62-77.

Garrad, Charles
309. 1964 "Fluted point from near London, Ontario". *Archaeological Society of Western Ontario, Bulletin*, Vol. 1, No. 1, pp. 8-11.

310. 1967 "A fluted point from Collingwood Township, Ontario". *Ontario Archaeology*, No. 10, pp. 29-33.

311. 1971 "Ontario fluted point survey". *Ontario Archaeology*, No. 16, pp. 3-18.

Gates, S.H.
312. 1961 "An archaeological survey of the DuPage River drainage". In, "Chicago area archaeology", *Illinois Archaeological Survey, Bulletin* 3, pp. 1-6.

Geikie, James
313. 1874 *The great ice age and its relation to the antiquity of man*. D. Appleton and Company, New York, 545 pp.

Gidley, James W.
314. 1926a "Fossil man associated with the mammoth in Florida: New evidence of the antiquity of man in America". *Washington Academy of Science, Journal*, Vol. 16, No. 11, p. 310.

315. 1926b "Fossil man in Florida". Abstract, *Geological Society of America, Bulletin*, Vol. 37, No. 1, pp. 239-240.

316. 1926c "Investigation of evidences of Early Man at Melbourne and Vero, Florida". *Smithsonian Miscellaneous Collection*, Vol. 78, No. 1, pp. 23-26.

317. 1927a "An elephant hunt in Florida". *Smithsonian Miscellaneous Collections*, Vol. 78, Article 7, pp. 48-51.

318. 1927b "Investigating evidence of Early Man in Florida". *Smithsonian Miscellaneous Collection*, Vol. 78, No. 7, pp. 168-174.

319. 1929a "Ancient man in Florida: Further investigations". *Geological Society of America, Bulletin*, Vol. 40, No. 2, pp. 491-501. Also, abstract, *Pan-American Geologist*, Vol. 51, No. 3, p. 236.

320. 1929b "Further study of the problem of Early Man in Florida". *Smithsonian Institute, Exploration and Field Work in 1928,* Publication No. 3011, pp. 13-20.

321. 1930 "Investigation of Early Man in Florida". *Smithsonian Institute, Exploration and Field Work in 1929*, pp. 37-38.

322. 1931 "Further investigations on evidences of Early Man in Florida". *Smithsonian Institute, Exploration and Field Work in 1930*, pp. 41-44.

Gidley, James W., and Frederic B. Loomis
323. 1926 "Fossil man in Florida". *American Journal of Science*, Fifth Series, Vol. *XII*, (Whole Number *CCXII*), No. 69, pp. 254-264.

Gilbert, G.K.
324. 1887 "On a prehistoric hearth under the quaternary deposits in western New York". *Scientific American Supplement*, Vol. 23, No. 577, p. 9221.

Gilliam, Charles Edgar
325. 1958 "Type Early Man graver, Williamson Site, Dinwiddie County". *Archeological Society of Virginia, Quarterly Bulletin*, Vol. 13, No. 1, pp. 8-9.

Gillis, Edward V. (Editor)
326. 1958 "Ancient skull". *The Coffinberry News Bulletin*, Vol. V, No. 6, Wright L. Coffinberry Chapter, Michigan Archaeological Society, Grand Rapids, p. 6.

327. 1959 "Paleo-Indian type points". *The Coffinberry News Bulletin*, Vol. VI, No. 3, Wright L. Coffinberry Chapter, Michigan Archaeological Society, Grand Rapids, p. 34.

328. 1960 "The Flat River Site No. 26, Kent Co., Mich." *The Coffinberry News Bulletin*, Vol. VII, No. 10, November, Wright L. Coffinberry Chapter, Michigan Archaeological Society, Grand Rapids, pp. 116-119.

Gillman, Henry
329. 1876 "The ancient men of the Great Lakes". Abstract, *Proceedings of the American Association for the Advancement of Science*, 24th Meet-

ing, held at Detroit, Michigan, August, 1875. Published by the Permanent Secretary, Salem, Massachusetts, pp. 316-322.

Girovard, Laurent
330. 1972 "Archéologie préhistorique au Québec . . . été 1971". *Recherches Amérindiennes au Québec, Bulletin d'information*, Vol. 11, No. 1, pp. 40-70.

Gleason, Kenneth
331. 1942 "A Folsom-like point". *Archaeological Society of New Jersey, Newsletter*, No. 7, p. 6.

Goodyear, Albert C.
332. 1968 "Pinellas Point: A possible site of continuous Indian habitation". *Florida Anthropologist*, Vol. 21, Nos. 2-3, pp. 74-82.

333. 1973 "Archaic hafted spokeshaves with graver spurs from the southeast". *Florida Anthropologist*, Vol. 26, No. 1, pp. 39-44.

Goodyear, Albert C., William Thompson, and Lyman O. Warren
334. 1968 "Suwannee style end scrapers from Pinellas County". *Florida Anthropologist*, Vol. 21, Nos. 2-3, p. 91.

Goodyear, Albert C., and Lyman O. Warren
335. 1972 "Further observations on the submarine oyster shell deposits of Tampa Bay". *Florida Anthropologist*, Vol. 25, No. 2, Part 1, pp. 52-66.

Goggin, John M.
336. 1949 "Cultural traditions in Florida prehistory". In, *The Florida Indian and his neighbors*, John W. Griffin (Editor). Winter Park, Florida, pp. 13-44.

337. 1950 "An early lithic complex from central Florida". *American Antiquity*, Vol. 16, No. 1, pp. 46-49.

338. 1952 "Space and time perspective in northern St. Johns archeology, Florida". *Yale University, Publications in Anthropology*, No. 47.

Gottlieb, F.W.
339. 1910 "Palaeolithic, Neolithic, Copper and Iron Ages of Shelby County, Indiana". *Proceedings of the Indiana Academy of Science*, Vol. 10, pp. 153-168.

Grasso, Dick Edgar Ibara
340. 1962 Comments on, "The Paleo-Indian tradition in eastern North America", by Ronald J. Mason. In, *Current Anthropology*, Vol. 3, No. 3, Chicago, pp. 254-255.

Green, Amos R.

341. 1963a "The Prillwitz mammoth". *The Coffinberry News Bulletin*, Vol. *X*, No. 2, February, Wright L. Coffinberry Chapter, Michigan Archaeological Society, Grand Rapids, pp. 15-18.

342. 1963b "The Prillwitz mammoth, Part *II*". *The Coffinberry News Bulletin*, Vol. *X*, No. 3, March, Wright L. Coffinberry Chapter, Michigan Archaeological Society, Grand Rapids, pp. 28-29.

343. 1967 "Paleo-Indian and mammoth were contemporaneous in Berrien County, Michigan". *Michigan Archaeologist*, Vol. 13, No. 1, pp. 1-10.

Greenman, Emerson F.

344. 1938 "Cultural relationships of archaeological sites in the Upper Great Lakes Region". *Papers of the Michigan Academy of Science, Arts, and Letters XXIV*, Part IV, pp. 1-10.

345. 1941a "Excavation of a prehistoric site in Manitoulin District, Ontario". *Man*, Vol. 41, Correspondence No. 56, Eyre and Spottiswoode Limited, His Majesty's Printers, London, pp. 67-68.

346. 1941b "Sites on abandoned beaches of Lake Huron, Ontario". Abstract, *Society for American Archaeology, Notebook*, Vol. 2, pp. 26-27

347. 1942 "Further excavations in Manitoulin District, Ontario". *Man*, Vol. 42, Correspondence No. 69, Eyre and Spottiswoode Limited, His Majesty's Printers, London, p. 119.

348. 1943a "Further excavations in Manitoulin District, Ontario; the chronology". *Man*, Vol. 43, Correspondence No. 32, Eyre and Spottiswoode Limited, His Majesty's Printers, London, p. 48.

349. 1943b "An early industry on a raised beach near Killarney, Ontario". *American Antiquity*, Vol. 8, No. 3, pp. 260-265.

350. 1948 "The Killarney sequence and its Old World connections". *Papers of the Michigan Academy of Science, Arts, and Letters*, Vol. 32, pp. 312-332.

351. 1950 "Early Man in America". *Antiquity*, Vol. 24, pp. 42-43.

352. 1955 "Wave action at George Lake I, Ontario". *American Antiquity*, Vol. 20, No. 4, pp. 376-377.

353. 1957 "An American Eolithic?" *American Antiquity*, Vol. 22, No. 3, p. 298.

354. 1960 "The North Atlantic and Early Man in the New World". *Michigan Archaeologist*, Vol. 6, pp. 19-39.

355. 1962 Comments on, "The Paleo-Indian tradition in eastern North America", by Ronald J. Mason. *Current Anthropology*, Vol. 3, No. 3, Chicago, pp. 252-254.

356. 1963 "The Upper Palaeolithic and the New World". *Current Anthropology*, Vol. 4, No. 1, pp. 41-91.

357. 1966 "Chronology of sites at Killarney, Canada". *American Antiquity*, Vol. 31, No. 4, pp. 540-551.

Greenman, Emerson F., James B. Griffin, and Albert C. Spaulding

358. 1956 "Notes on the prehistory of the Upper Great Lakes area". *Friends of the Pleistocene Guidebook, Midwest Section*, mimeographed, Ann Arbor, pp. 30-33.

Greenman, Emerson F., and George M. Stanley

359. 1940 "A geologically dated camp site, Georgian Bay, Ontario". *American Antiquity*, Vol. 5, No. 3, pp. 194-199.

360. 1943 "The archaeology and geology of two early sites near Killarney, Ontario". *Papers of the Michigan Academy of Science, Arts, and Letters*, Vol. 28, pp. 505-531.

Griffin, James B.

361. 1946 "Cultural change and continuity in eastern United States archaeology". In, *Man in northeastern North America*, Frederick Johnson (Editor), *Papers of the Robert S. Peabody Foundation for Archaeology*, Vol. 3, pp. 37-95.

Griffin, James B. (Editor)

362. 1952a *Archeology of eastern United States*. The University of Chicago Press, Chicago, 392 pp., 205 figures.

Griffin, James B.

363. 1952b "Prehistoric cultures of the central Mississippi Valley". In, *Archeology of eastern United States*, James B. Griffin (Editor). The University of Chicago Press, Chicago, pp. 226-238.

364. 1952c "Culture periods in eastern United States archeology". In, *Archeology of eastern United States*, James B. Griffin (Editor), The University of Chicago Press, Chicago, pp. 352-364.

365. 1952d "Radiocarbon dates for the eastern United States". In, *Archeology of eastern United States*, James B. Griffin (Editor), The University of Chicago Press, Chicago, pp. 365-370.

366. 1956a "The reliability of radiocarbon dates for late glacial and recent times in central and eastern North America". In, Papers of the Third Great Basin Archaeological Conference, Robert Anderson (Editor), *University of Utah Anthropological Papers* 26, pp. 10-34.

367. 1956b "Prehistoric settlement patterns in the northern Mississippi Valley and the Upper Great Lakes". In, *Prehistoric Settlement Patterns in the New World*, Gordon R. Willey (Editor), Viking Fund Publications in Anthropology, No. 23, pp. 63-72.

368. 1961 "Post-glacial ecology and culture changes in the Great Lakes area of North America". *University of Michigan Great Lakes Research Division, Publication* No. 7, pp. 147-155.

369. 1964 "The northeast Woodlands area". In, *Prehistoric Man in the New World*, Jesse D. Jennings and Edward Norbeck (Editors), University of Chicago Press, Chicago, pp. 223-258.

370. 1965 "Late quaternary prehistory in the northeastern Woodlands". In, *The quaternary of the United States*, H.E. Wright, Jr., and D.G. Frey (Editors), Princeton University Press, Princeton, New Jersey, pp. 655-667.

371. 1967 "Eastern North American archaeology: A summary". *Science,* Vol. 156, pp. 175-191.

372. 1968 "Observation on Illinois prehistory in late Pleistocene and early recent times". In, *The Quaternary of Illinois*, Robert E. Bergstrom (Editor), *University of Illinois, College of Agriculture, Special Publication* No. 14, Urbana, Illinois, pp. 123-137.

Griffin, John W.
373. 1952a "Early hunters of Florida". *Florida Wildlife*, Vol. 5, No. 10, pp. 20-21, 34-35.

374. 1952b "Prehistoric Florida: A Review". In, *Archeology of eastern United States*, James B. Griffin (Editor), The University of Chicago Press, Chicago, pp. 322-334.

Grimsley, Tom
375. 1969 "Happiness: Finding a rare Paleo point". *Central States Archaeological Journal*, Vol. 16, No. 3, pp. 126-127.

Guilday, John E.
376. 1968 "Archaeological evidence of caribou from New York and Massachusetts". *Journal of Mammalogy*, Vol. 49, No. 2, pp. 344-345.

377. 1969 "A possible caribou-Paleo-Indian association from Dutchess Quarry Cave, Orange County, New York". *New York State Archeological Association, The Bulletin*, Number 45, pp. 24-29.

378. 1972 Introductory remarks to "Mice, men and mastadons", by Richard S. Mills. In, *The Explorer*, Vol. 14, No. 2, p. 9.

Guilday, John E., P.S. Martin, and A.D. McCrady

379. 1964 "New Paris No. 4: A late Pleistocene cave deposit in Bedford County, Pennsylvania". *National Speleological Society, Bulletin*, Vol. 26, No. 4, pp. 121-194.

Gustafson, John H.

380. 1972 "An unfinished fluted point and review of fluted-point technology". *Journal of Alabama Archaeology*, Vol. 18, No. 1, pp. 47-54.

Guthe, Alfred K.

381. 1956 Review of, *Prehistory of the Upper Ohio Valley; An introductory archeological study*, by William J. Mayer-Oakes. In, *New York State Archeological Association, The Bulletin*, No. 7, pp. 14-15.

382. 1958 "The late prehistoric occupation in southwestern New York: An interpretive analysis". *Researches and Transactions of the New York State Archeological Association*, Vol. XIV, No. 1, 100 pp.

383. 1961a "The Stanfield-Worley rock shelter". *Tennessee Archaeologist*, Vol. 17, No. 2, pp. 54-55.

384. 1961b "Clovis points". *Tennessee Archaeologist*, Vol. 17, No. 2, pp. 56-58.

385. 1961c "A Cumberland variant". *Tennessee Archaeologist*, Vol. 17, No. 2, p. 58.

386. 1961d "Fluted point". *Tennessee Archaeologist*, Vol. 17, No. 2, p. 59.

387. 1962a "Paleo-Indian material". *Tennessee Archaeologist*, Vol. 17, No. 1, pp. 52-55.

388. 1962b "Fluted points in the Burbage collection". *Tennessee Archaeologist*, Vol. 17, No. 1, pp. 56-57.

389. 1962c "Editors' notes" (Illustration of two Cumberland points). *Tennessee Archaeologist*, Vol. 18, No. 2, p. 101.

390. 1963a "From the L.L. Smith collection". *Tennessee Archaeologist*, Vol. 19, No. 1, p. 25.

391. 1963b "Editors' notes" (Clovis points). *Tennessee Archaeologist*, Vol. 19, No. 1, pp. 26-27.

392. 1963c "Ernest J. Sims' collection". *Tennessee Archaeologist*, Vol. 19, No. 2, pp. 62-69.

393. 1964a "Two early projectile points from Greene County". *Tennessee Archaeologist*, Vol. 20, No. 1, p. 47.

394. 1964b "A reworked Clovis point". *Tennessee Archaeologist*, Vol. 20, No. 2, p. 83.

395. 1964c "The Tip Bowden collection", and "Points from east Tennessee". *Tennessee Archaeologist*, Vol. 20, No. 2, pp. 84-88.

396. 1965a "Paleo-Indian projectile points". *Tennessee Archaeologist*, Vol. 21, No. 1, pp. 28-33.

397. 1965b "Paleo-Indian points from east Tennessee". *Tennessee Archaeoligist*, Vol. 21, No. 2, pp. 72-75.

398. 1965c Review of, *Paleo-Indian culture in Kentucky*, by Martha A. Rolingson. In, *American Anthropologist*, Vol. 67, No. 1, pp. 162-163.

399. 1966a "Editors' Notes" (Description of four Paleo-Indian projectile points). *Tennessee Archaeologist*, Vol. 22, No. 1, p. 46.

400. 1966b "Tennessee's Paleo-Indian". *Tennessee Archaeologist*, Vol. 22, No. 2, pp. 67-77.

401. 1966c "Paleo-Indian points from middle Tennessee". *Tennessee Archaeologist*, Vol. 22, No. 2, p. 80.

402. 1966d "Paleo-Indian points from Hardin County". *Tennessee Archeologist*, Vol. 22, No. 2, pp. 81-83.

403. 1967a "Two Cumberland points from middle Tennessee" and "Additional Paleo-Indian points from east Tennessee". *Tennessee Archaeologist*, Vol. 23, No. 1, pp. 42-44.

404. 1967b "Early projectile point types in North Carolina". *Tennessee Archaeologist*, Vol. 23, No. 2, p. 84.

405. 1967c "The Paleo-Indian of Tennessee". *Eastern States Archeological Federation, Bulletin*, No. 26, p. 11.

406. 1969 "Early projectile points from middle Tennessee". *Tennessee Archaeologist*, Vol. 25, No. 1, pp. 24-35.

407. 1970 "Fluted points". *Tennessee Archaeologist*, Vol. 26, No. 1, pp. 20-22.

Hadlock, Wendell S., and Douglas S. Byers
408. 1956 "Radiocarbon dates from Ellsworth Falls, Maine". *American Antiquity*, "Facts and Comments", Vol. 21, No. 4, pp. 419-420.

Haight, Marion, and Norman L. Wright,
409. 1966 "Reworked Palaeo artifacts". *Ohio Archaeologist*, Vol. 16, p. 74

Hahn, Richard N. (Mrs.)

410. 1966 "New Dalton-Big Sandy distribution". *Journal of Alabama Archaeology*, Vol. 12, No. 1, pp. 70-71.

Halbert, H.S.

411. 1909 "The archaeology of the Gulf region east of the Mississippi River". *American Anthropologist*, Vol. 11, pp. 495-496.

Hall, James

412. 1871 "Notes and observations on the Cohoes mastadon". *Twenty-first Annual Report, University of the State of New York*, pp. 99-145.

Hall, Roland Scott

413. 1952 "Early Man site in Canada". *Oklahoma Anthropological Society, Newsletter*, Vol. 1, No. 6, pp. 3-5.

Hay, Oliver P.

414. 1917a "On the finding of supposed Pleistocene human remains at Vero, Florida". *Washington Academy of Science, Journal*, Vol. 7, No. 11, pp. 358-360.

415. 1917b "The quaternary deposits at Vero, Florida, and the vertebrate remains contained therein". *Journal of Geology*, Vol. 25, No. 1, pp. 52-55.

416. 1917c "Vertebrata mostly from stratum no. 3, at Vero, Florida, together with descriptions of new species". *Florida Geological Survey, Ninth Annual Report*, pp. 43-68.

417. 1918a "A review of some papers on fossil man at Vero, Florida". *Science*, N.S., Vol. 47, pp. 370-371.

418. 1918b "Doctor Ales Hrdlicka and the Vero man". *Science*, N.S., Vol. 48, No. 1245, pp. 459-462.

419. 1918c "Further consideration of the occurrence of human remains in the Pleistocene deposits at Vero, Florida". *American Anthropologist*, N.S., Vol. 20, No. 1, pp. 1-36.

420. 1919 "On Pleistocene man at Trenton, New Jersey". *Anthropological Scraps*, No. 2, pp. 5-8.

421. 1921 "The newest discovery of 'ancient' man in the United States". *Anthropological Scraps*, No. 4, pp. 13-16.

422. 1923 "The Pleistocene of North America and its vertebrated animals from the states east of the Mississippi River and from the Canadian provinces east of Longitude 95°". *Carnegie Institution of Washington, Publication* No. 322, Washington, D.C., pp. 38-39, 122-123, 159-160, 163-199, 208, 222, 233, 263, 373, 379.

423. 1926 "On the geological age of Pleistocene vertebrates found at Vero and Melbourne, Florida". *Washington Academy of Science, Journal*, Vol. 16, No. 14, pp. 387-392.

424. 1927 "A review of recent reports on investigations made in Florida on Pleistocene geology and paleontology". *Washington Academy of Science, Journal*, Vol. 17, No. 11, pp. 277-283.

425. 1928 "Again on Pleistocene man at Vero, Florida". *Washington Academy of Science, Journal*, Vol. 18, No. 9, pp. 233-241.

Hayes, Seth

426. 1895 "An examination and description of mastadon and accompanying mammalian remains found near Cincinnati". *Journal of Cincinnati Society of Natural History*, Vol. 17, pp. 217-226.

Haynes, C. Vance, Jr.

427. 1964 "Fluted projectile points: Their age and dispersion". *Science*, Vol. 145, No. 3639, pp. 1408-1413.

428. 1966 "Carbon-14 dates and Early Man in the New World". Proceedings of the Sixth International Conference on Radiocarbon and Tritium Dating, *U.S. Atomic Energy Commission Report*, Conference 650652, Paper 15, Washington, pp. 145-164.

429. 1967 "Carbon-14 dates and Early Man in the New World". In, *Pleistocene extinctions: The search for a cause*, P.S. Martin and H.E. Wright, Jr. (Editors). Volume 6 of the Proceedings of the *VII* Congress of the International Association for Quaternary Research, Yale University Press, New Haven and London, pp. 267-286.

430. 1969 "The earliest Americans". *Science*, Vol. 166, No. 3906, pp. 709-715.

431. 1970 "Geochronology of man-mammoth sites and their bearing on the origin of the Llano Complex". In, *Pleistocene and recent environments of the central Great Plains*, Wakefield Dort, Jr., and J. Knox Jones, Jr., (Editors). Department of Geology, University of Kansas, Special Publication 3, Part 2—Anthropology, University Press of Kansas, pp. 77-92.

432. 1971 "Time, environment, and Early Man". *Arctic Anthropology*, Vol. *VIII*, No. 2, pp. 3-14.

Haynes, Henry Williamson

433. 1883 "The argillite implements found in the gravels of the Delaware River at Trenton, New Jersey, compared with the Paleolithic implements of Europe". *Proceedings of the Boston Society of Natural History*, pp. 132-137.

434. 1893a "The Palaeolithic man in Ohio". *Science,* Vol. 21, p. 291.

435. 1893b "Early Man in Minnesota". *Science,* Vol. 21, pp. 318-319.

436. 1893c "Early Man in Minnesota". *The Archaeologist,* Vol. 1, pp. 144-146.

Harp, Elmer, Jr.
437. 1951 "An archaeological survey in the Strait of Belle Isle area". *American Antiquity,* Vol. 16, No. 3, pp. 203-220.

Harrington, Mark Raymond
438. 1933 "Gypsum Cave, Nevada". *Southwest Museum Papers,* No. 8, 197 pp.

Hasse, Brian
439. 1969 "A survey of sites in central Carver County, Minnesota". *Minnesota Archaeologist,* Vol. 30, No. 1, pp. 3-27.

Hatt, Robert T.
440. 1963 "The mastadon of Pontiac". *Cranbrook Institute of Science, News Letter,* Vol. 32, No. 6, Bloomfield Hills, Michigan, pp. 62-64.

Heilprin, Angelo
441. 1887 "Exploration on the west coast of Florida". *Transactions of the Wagner Free Institute of Science,* Vol. 1, pp. 14-15.

Helton, O.P.
442. 1895 "Paleolithic implements". In, "Collector's department", *The Archaeologist,* Vol. III, No. 6, Official Organ of the Ohio Archaeological and Historical Society, Columbus, Ohio, pp 208-211.

Hemmings, E. Thomas
443. 1972 "Early Man in the South Atlantic States". Abstract of a paper given at the 1971 annual meeting of the Eastern States Archeological Federation. *Eastern States Archeological Federation,* Bulletin 31, pp. 10-11.

Henry, John, and Al Nichols
444. 1963 "Paleo-points from Vermillion County, Illinois". *Reports on Illinois Prehistory I, Illinois Archaeological Survey,* Bulletin 4, pp. 119-125.

Hester, James J.
445. 1960 "Late Pleistocene extinction and radiocarbon dating". *American Antiquity,* Vol. 26, No. 1, pp. 58-77.

446. 1967 "The agency of man in animal extinctions". In, *Pleistocene extinctions: The search for a cause,* P.S. Martin and H.E. Wright, Jr.

(Editors). Volume 6 of the Proceedings of the *VII* Congress of the International Association for Quaternary Research. Yale University Press, New Haven and London, pp. 169-192.

447. 1970 "Ecology of the North American Paleo-Indian". *BioScience*, Vol. 20, No. 4, pp. 213-217.

Hibbard, C.W.

448. 1958 "Occurrence of the extinct moose, *Cervales*, in the Pleistocene of Michigan". *Michigan Academy of Science, Arts, and Letters Papers*, Vol. 43, pp. 33-37.

Hill, M.W.

449. 1950 "Yuma-type points". *Tennessee Archaeologist*, "Communications", Vol. *VI*, No. 1, p. 11.

450. 1951 "Early projectile forms". *Tennessee Archaeologist*, Vol. *VII*, No. 1, pp. 22-23.

451. 1952a "Accidental fluting". *Tennessee Archaeologist*, Vol. *VIII*, No. 1, pp. 16-17.

452. 1952b "Unfluted Folsom-like points". *Tennessee Archaeologist*, Vol. *VIII*, No. 1, pp. 17-18.

453. 1952c "Observations upon early flints of pentagonal form". *Tennessee Archaeologist*, Vol. *VIII*, No. 1, pp. 18-21.

454. 1953 "What was the purpose of the single shouldered Yuma blade?" *Tennessee Archaeologist*, Vol. *IX*, No. 1, pp. 22-23.

Hiller, Wesley R.

455. 1939 "The Minnesota man". *Minnesota Archaeologist*, Vol. 5, p. 52.

Holland, C.G.

456. 1960 "Preceramic and ceramic cultural patterns in northwest Virginia". *Bureau of American Ethnology, Bulletin* 173, *Anthropological Papers*, No. 57, pp. 1-129.

457. 1970 "An archeological survey of southwest Virginia". *Smithsonian Contributions to Anthropology*, No. 12, 194 pp.

Hollick, Arthur

458. 1897 "A new investigation of man's antiquity at Trenton". *Science*, N.S., Vol. 6, pp. 675-682.

459. 1898 Appendix to "A new investigation of man's antiquity at Trenton", by H.C. Mercer. *Proceedings of the American Association for the Advancement of Science, for 1897*, Vol. 46, pp. 378-381.

Holmes, William Henry

460. n.d. "Are there traces of glacial man in the Trenton gravels". *Winsor Collection, Paper,* Vol. 3, No. 4.

461. 1892 "Modern quarry refuse and Palaeolithic theory". *Science,* 2nd. Series, Vol. 20, pp. 295-297.

462. 1893a "Are there traces of glacial man in the Trenton Gravels?" *Journal of Geology,* Vol. 1, pp. 15-37.

463. 1893b "Traces of glacial man in Ohio". *Journal of Geology,* Vol. 1, pp. 147-163.

464. 1893c "Vestiges of Early Man in Minnesota". *American Geologist,* Vol. 11, pp. 219-240.

465. 1893d "On the so-called Palaeolithic implements of the upper Mississippi". *Proceedings of the American Association for the Advancement of Science for 1892,* Vol. 41, pp. 280-281.

466. 1893e "Traces of glacial man in Ohio". *The Archaeologist,* Vol. 1, pp. 163-170.

467. 1897 "Stone implements of the Potomac-Chesapeake Tidewater Province". *Fifteenth Annual Report of the Bureau of Ethnology to the Secretary of the Smithsonian Institution, 1893-'94,* Washington, pp. 3-152.

468. 1898 "Primitive man in the Delaware Valley". *Proceedings of the American Association for the Advancement of Science, for 1897,* Vol. 46, pp. 364-370.

469. 1902a "Flint implements and fossil remains from a sulphur spring at Afton, Indian Territory". *American Anthropologist,* N.S., Vol. 4, pp. 108-129.

470. 1918 "On the antiquity of man in America". *Science,* N.S., Vol. 47, No. 1223, pp. 561-562.

471. 1919 "Handbook of Aboriginal American antiquities. Part *I*, Introductory, The lithic industries". *Bureau of American Ethnology, Bulletin* 60, Washington, D.C., 380 pp.

472. 1925 "The antiquity phantom in American archeology". *Science,* N.S., Vol. *LXII,* No. 1603, pp. 256-258.

Hooper, A.B., *III*

473. 1968 "Pebble tools: Lively complex duplicated in Bear Creek watershed". *Journal of Alabama Archaeology,* Vol. 14, No. 1, pp. 1-16

474. 1969 "Three finger technology: Holding pebble tools". *Journal of Alabama Archaeology*, Vol. 15, No. 2, pp. 48-58.

Hopkins, David M.
475. 1962 Comments on, "The Paleo-Indian tradition in eastern North America", by Ronald J. Mason. In, *Current Anthropology*, Vol. 3, No. 3, Chicago, p. 254.

Hough, Jack L.
476. 1958 *Geology of the Great Lakes.* University of Illinois Press, 313 pp.

477. 1963 "The prehistoric Great Lakes of North America". *American Scientist*, Vol. 51, No. 1, pp. 84-109.

478. 1966 "Correlation of glacial lake stages in the Huron-Erie and Michigan basins". *Geology*, Vol. 74, pp. 62-77.

Howard, Edgar B.
479. 1934 "Grooved spearpoints". *Pennsylvania Archaeologist, Bulletin*, Vol. 3, No. 6, pp. 11-15.

480. 1935 "Evidence of Early Man in North America". *Pennsylvania University Museum Journal*, Vol. 24, Nos. 2-3, Philadelphia.

481. 1936a "Early Man in America". *American Philosophical Society*, Vol. 76, No. 3, pp. 327-333.

482. 1936b "An outline of the problem of man's antiquity in North America". *American Anthropologist*, N.S., Vol. 38, pp. 394-413.

483. 1936c "Studies of Early Man". *Carnegie Institution of Washington, Year Book*, No. 35, p. 323.

484. 1937 "The Folsom problem in North America". *Zeitschrift für Rassenkunde*, Band 6, Heft 3, pp. 331-336.

485. 1940 "Studies bearing upon the problem of Early Man in Florida". *Carnegie Institution of Washington Year Book*, No. 39, pp. 309-312.

486. 1942 "A 'fluted point' site in Pennsylvania". *Pennsylvania Archaeologist*, Vol. 12, pp. 4-6.

487. 1943 "The Finley Site: Discovery of Yuma points, in situ, near Eden, Wyoming". *American Antiquity*, Vol. 8, No. 3, pp. 224-234.

Howells, W.W.
488. 1938 "Crania from Wyoming resembling 'Minnesota man'". *American Antiquity*, Vol. 3, No. 4, pp. 318-326.

Hrdlička, Aleš

489. 1902 "The crania of Trenton, New Jersey". *American Museum of Natural History Bulletin*, Vol. 16, pp. 23-62.

490. 1907 "Skeletal remains suggesting or attributed to Early Man in North America". *Bureau of American Ethnology, Bulletin* 33, Washington, D.C., 113 pp.

491. 1911 "A report on the Trenton femur", published with E. Volk, "The archeology of the Delaware Valley". *Memoirs of the Peabody Museum*, V, Cambridge, Massachusetts, pp. 244-247.

492. 1912 "Early Man in America". *American Journal of Science*, Fourth Series, Vol. XXXIV, (Whole Number CLXXXIV), No. 204, pp. 543-554

493. 1917 "Preliminary report on finds of supposedly ancient human remains at Vero, Florida". *Journal of Geology*, Vol. 25, No. 1, pp. 43-51

494. 1918 "Recent discoveries attributed to Early Man in America". *Bureau of American Ethnology, Bulletin* 66, Washington, D.C. 67 pp.

495. 1919 "Examination of ancient human remains in Florida". *Smithsonian Institution Annual Report, 1917*, pp. 10-12.

496. 1937a "Early Man in America: What have the bones to say?" In, *Early Man: As depicted by leading authorities at the International Symposium, The Academy of Natural Sciences, Philadelphia, March 1937*, George Grant MacCurdy (Editor). Introduction by John C. Merriam. J.B. Lippincott Company, London, pp. 93-104.

497. 1937b "The Minnesota 'man' ". *American Journal of Physical Anthropology*, Vol. 22, No. 2, pp. 175-199.

498. 1942 "The problem of man's antiquity in America". *Proceedings of the 8th American Science Congress*, Vol. 2, pp. 53-55.

Hue, E.

499. 1918 "L'homme fossile de Vero, Floride, Etats-Unis". *Société Préhistorique française, Bulletin*, t. XV, pp. 319-336.

Humbard, R.A.

500. 1967 "Quartzite pebble tools". *Journal of Alabama Archaeology*, Vol. 13, No. 1, pp. 52-55.

Hurley, William M.

501. 1965 "Archaeological research in the projected Kickapoo Reservoir, Vernon County, Wisconsin". *Wisconsin Archeologist*, Vol. 46, No. 1, pp. 1-113.

Hurley, William M., and Ian T. Kenyon

502. 1970 "Algonquin Park archaeology, 1970". *Research Report* No. 5, *Department of Anthropology, University of Toronto*, 174 pp.

Hurt, Wesley R., Jr.

503. 1949 "Resemblances between the pre-ceramic horizons of the southeast and southwest". Paper read at the 14th Annual Meeting of the Society for American Archaeology, Bloomington, Indiana, May 13.

504. 1953 "A comparative study of the preceramic occupation of North America". *American Antiquity*, Vol. 18, No. 3, pp. 204-222.

Hyde, E.W.

505. 1960 "Mid-Ohio Valley Paleo-Indian and suggested sequence of the fluted point cultures". *West Virginia Archeological Society, Special Publication* 5.

Imbelloni, José

506. 1943 "The peopling of America". *Acta American*, Vol. 1, pp. 309-330.

Imel, Ivan

507. 1969 "Reflections on fluted points". *Central States Archaeological Journal*, Vol. 16, No. 2, pp. 88-93.

Irving, William N.

508. 1971 "Recent Early Man research in the north". *Arctic Anthropology*, Vol. VIII, No. 2, pp. 68-82.

Jackson, George A.

509. 1940 "Rare Folsom point found near Nebo". *Archeological Society of Connecticut, News-letter*, No. 9, pp. 1-2.

Jelinek, Arthur J.

510. 1957 "Pleistocene faunas and Early Man". *Papers of Michigan Academy of Science, Arts and Letters*, Vol. 42, 1956, pp. 225-237.

511. 1962 Comments on, "The Paleo-Indian tradition in eastern North America", by Ronald J. Mason. In, *Current Anthropology*, Vol. 3, No. 3, Chicago, pp. 255-256.

512. 1962 "An index of radiocarbon dates associated with cultural materials". *Current Anthropology*, Vol. 3, No. 5, pp. 451-477.

513. 1965 "The Upper Paleolithic revolution and the peopling of the New World". *Michigan Archaeologist*, Vol. 11, Nos. 3-4, pp. 85-88.

514. 1971 "Early Man in the New World: A technological perspective". *Arctic Anthropology*, Vol. VIII, No. 2, pp. 15-21.

Jenks, Albert Ernest

515. 1932a "Minnesota Pleistocene Homo". Summary in, *Science*, N.S., Vol. 76, pp. 546-547.

516. 1932b "Pleistocene man in Minnesota". *Science*, N.S., Vol. 75, pp. 607-608.

517. 1932c "The problem of the culture from the Arvilla gravel pit". *American Anthropologist*, N.S., Vol. 34, pp. 455-466.

518. 1932d "Minnesota's glacial-age 'man'; skeleton found in 20,000-year-old lake bed near Pelican Rapids is that of a woman, but it is designated as 'the Minnesota man' by anthropologists. Discovery indicates presence of glacial-age men in western Minnesota". *Minneapolis Journal*, Editorial Section, Sunday, December 18, p. 6.

519. 1933 "Minnesota Pleistocene Homo, an interim communication". *Proceedings of the National Academy of Science*, Vol. 19, No. 1, pp. 1-6.

520. 1934 "The discovery of an ancient Minnesota maker of Yuma and Folsom flints". *Science*, N.S., Vol. 80, p. 205.

521. 1935 "Recent discoveries in Minnesota prehistory". *Minnesota History*, Vol. 16, pp. 1-21.

522. 1936 *Pleistocene Man in Minnesota*. University of Minnesota Press, Minneapolis, 197 pp.

523. 1937 "Minnesota's Browns Valley man and associated burial artifacts". *Memoirs of the American Anthropological Association*, No. 49, Menasha, Wisconsin, 49 pp.

524. 1938 "Minnesota man: A reply to a review by Dr. Aleš Hrdlička". *American Anthropologist*, N.S., Vol. 40, pp. 328-336.

525. 1939 "Prehistoric Minnesotan". (In Re-"America" . . . Minneapolis, Vol. 1, p. 8.)

Jenks, Albert Ernest and H.H. Simpson, Sr..

526. 1941 "Beveled artifacts in Florida of the same type as artifacts found near Clovis, New Mexico". *American Antiquity*, Vol. 6, No. 4, pp. 314-319.

Jennings, Jesse D. and Edward Norbeck (Editors)

527. 1964 *Prehistoric man in the New World*. University of Chicago Press, Chicago.

Jillson, Willard Rouse
528. 1969 "Discovery of a late Glacio-Lacustrine vertebrate fauna at Frankfort, Kentucky". Roberts Printing Company, Frankfort, Kentucky, 17 pp.

Johnson, Elden
529. 1969 "The prehistoric peoples of Minnesota". *Minnesota Prehistoric Archaeology Series,* Minnesota Historical Society, St. Paul, 26 pp.

Johnson, Frederick
530. 1951 "Radiocarbon dating". *American Antiquity,* Vol. 17, No. 1, Part 2, Memoir 8, 65 pp.

Johnson Frederick (Editor)
531. 1956 *Chronology and development of early cultures in North America.* Andover, Massachusetts.

Johnson, Frederick, and O.J. Neill
532. 1961 "Some ancient sites in Greensberg and Ottawa Townships, Putnam County, Ohio". *American Antiquity,* Vol. 26, No. 3, pp. 420-426.

Johnson, Ludwell H., III
533. 1952 "Men and elephants in America". *Scientific Monthly,* Vol. 75, No. 4, pp. 215-220.

Johnston, Richard B.
534. 1968 "Archaeology of Rice Lake, Ontario". *National Museum of Canada, Anthropology Papers,* No. 19, 49 pp.

Johnston, W.A.
535. 1933 "Quaternary geology of North America in relation to the migration of man". In, *The American Aborigines, their origin and antiquity,* Diamond Jenness (Editor), Fifth Pacific Science Congress, Canada, University of Toronto Press, Toronto, pp. 9-45.

Jolly, Fletcher, III
536. 1970 "Fluted points reworked by later peoples". *Tennessee Archaeologist,* Vol. 26, No. 2, pp. 30-44.

Jordan, Douglas F.
537. 1956 "A Clovis point from Sullivan County". *Tennessee Archaeologist,* Vol. 12, No. 1, pp. 15-16.

538. 1969 "Early Man in New England". In, *An introduction to the archaeology and history of the Connecticut Valley Indian,* William R. Young (Editor), Museum of Science, Springfield, N.S., Vol. *I,* No. 1, pp. 11-15.

Josselyn, Daniel W.

539. 1952 "Ground-base projectile points". *Tennessee Archaeologist*, Vol. VIII, No. 3, pp. 65-72.

540. 1954 "Two new fluted point characteristics". *Tennessee Archaeologist*, Vol. X, No. 2, pp. 59-62.

541. 1963a "Method for classification of projectile points; Part 3, projectile point genetics". *Anthropological Journal of Canada*, Vol. 1, No. 2, pp. 17-20.

542. 1963b "Part 4: What is a projectile point type?" *Anthropological Journal of Canada*, Vol. 1, No. 2, pp. 21-24.

543. 1963c "Method for classification of projectile points: Part 5, Identification of typed projectile points". *Anthropological Journal of Canada*, Vol. 1, No. 3, pp. 11-14.

544. 1964a "Paleo-transitional projectile points, North Alabama". *New World Antiquity*, Vol. II, No. 1/2, pp. 19-22.

545. 1964b "The Paleo in Alabama: Summary, prospectus, bibliography". *New World Antiquity*, Vol. II, No. 9/10, pp. 106-116.

546. 1965a "America's 'crude tools'". *Tennessee Archaeologist*, Vol. 21, No. 2, pp. 55-66.

547. 1965b "'Ears' on Paleo points". *Anthropological Journal of Canada*, Vol. 3, No. 2, pp. 24-27.

548. 1966 "Announcing accepted American pebble tools—The Lively complex of Alabama". *Anthropological Journal of Canada*, Vol. 4, No. 1, pp. 24-31.

549. 1967a "Does America have a 'hand axe'?" *Anthropological Journal of Canada*, Vol. 5, No. 1, pp. 27-29.

550. 1967b "Pebble-tool terminology". *Anthropological Journal of Canada*, Vol. 5, No. 2, pp. 14-15.

551. 1967c "The pebble tool explosion in Alabama". *Anthropological Journal of Canada*, Vol. 5, No. 3, pp. 9-12.

552. 1967d "More on America's 'crude tools'". *Tennessee Archaeologist*, Vol. 23, No. 1, pp. 1-11.

553. 1968 "Too much Paleo". *Anthropological Journal of Canada*, Vol. 6, No. 4, pp. 10-15.

554. 1971 "Second time around". *Anthropological Journal of Canada*, Vol. 9, No. 2, pp. 2-6.

Josselyn, Daniel W. and Ernest H. Williams Jr.
555. 1970 "Fluting attempt". *Journal of Alabama Archaeology*, "Facts and Comments", Vol. 16, No. 2, pp. 135-136.

Karklins, Karlis
556. 1970 "The Fish Creek site, Hillsborough County, Florida". *Florida Anthropologist*, Vol. 23, No. 2, pp. 62-80.

Kay, George F.
557. 1939 "Pleistocene history and Early Man in America". *Geological Society of America, Bulletin*, Vol. 50, No. 3, pp. 453-463.

Kay, George F., and Morris M. Leighton
558. 1938 "Geological notes on the occurrence of 'Minnesota man'". *Journal of Geology*, Vol. 46, No. 3, Part I, pp. 268-278.

Kelley, B.E.
559. 1950 "Pre-glacial man in Ohio". *Ohio Indian Relic Collectors Society, Bulletin*, No. 24, pp. 34-35.

Kenyon, Walter A.
560. 1973 *A bibliography of Ontario archaeology*. Office of the Chief Archaeologist, Royal Ontario Museum, Toronto, Canada, mimeographed, 72 pp.

Kerby, M.D.
561. 1970a "Paleolithic tools in Virginia". *Archeological Society of Virginia, Quarterly Bulletin*, Vol. 24, No. 4, p. 251.

562. 1970b "Occurrence of artifacts in Old World Paleolithic forms". *Archeological Society of Virginia, Quarterly Bulletin*, Vol. 24, No. 4, p. 252.

Kidd, Kenneth E.
563. 1951 "Fluted points in Ontario". *American Antiquity*, Vol. 16, No. 3, p. 260.

564. 1952 "Sixty years of Ontario archeology". In, *Archeology of eastern United States*, James B. Griffin (Editor), University of Chicago Press, Chicago, pp. 71-82.

Kier, Charles F., Jr.
565. 1947 "The Jasper quarries at Vera Cruz, Pennsylvania". *Archaeological Society of Delaware, Bulletin*, Vol. 4, No. 4, pp. 22-26.

Kinsey, W. Fred, III

566. 1956 "A fluted-point fragment". *Pennsylvania Archaeologist*, Vol. 26, Nos. 3-4, p. 181.

567. 1958 "A survey of fluted points found in the Susquehanna Basin. Report No. 1". *Pennsylvania Archaeologist*, Vol. XXVIII, Nos. 3-4, pp. 103-111, 126.

568. 1959 "A survey of fluted points found in the Susquehanna Basin: Report No. 2". *Pennsylvania Archaeologist*, Vol. 29, No. 2, pp. 73-79.

Klammer, Paul

569. 1941 "Another sugar quartz Folsom from Minnesota". *Minnesota Archaeologist*, Vol. 7, p. 97.

Kleine, Harold K.

570. 1953 "A remarkable Paleo-Indian site in Alabama". *Tennessee Archaeologist*, Vol. 9, pp. 31-37.

Knapp, George N.

571. 1898 "On the implement-bearing sand deposits at Trenton". *Proceedings of the American Association for the Advancement of Science*, Vol. 46, 1897, p. 350.

Kneberg, Madeline

572. 1952 "The Tennessee area". In, *Archeology of eastern United States*, James B. Griffin (Editor). The University of Chicago Press, Chicago, pp. 190-198.

573. 1956 "Some important projectile point types found in the Tennessee area". *Tennessee Archaeologist*, Vol. 12, No. 1, pp. 17-28.

574. 1957 "Chipped stone artifacts of the Tennessee Valley area". *Tennessee Archaeologist*, Vol. 13, No. 1, pp. 55-66.

Knowles, Nathaniel

575. 1941 "Cultural stratification on the Trenton Bluff". *American Anthropologist*, N.S., Vol. 43, pp. 610-616.

Koch, A.K.

576. 1839 "Evidences of the contemporaneous existence of man with mastodon in Missouri". *Philadelphia Presbyterian*, January 12, 1839. Reprinted in, *American Journal of Science and Arts*, Vol. 36, pp. 191-192, 1839, and in, *Idem*, Third series, Vol. 9, pp. 338-339, 1875.

577. 1857 "Mastodon remains, in the State of Missouri, together with evidence of the existence of man contemporaneously with the mastodon". *Transactions of the Academy of Science of St. Louis*, Vol. 1, pp. 61-64.

Kraft, Herbert
578. 1971 "A preliminary report on the first Paleo Indian occupation sites in New Jersey". Abstract, *Eastern States Archeological Federation, Bulletin* 30, p. 14.

Krantz, Grover S.
579. 1970 "Human activities and megafaunal extinctions". *American Scientist*, Volume 58, No. 2, pp. 164-170.

Krieger, Alex D.
580. 1947 "Certain projectile points of the early American hunters". *Texas Archeological and Paleontological Society, Bulletin*, Vol. 18, Lubbock, Texas, pp. 7-27.

581. 1950 "Suggested general sequence in North American projectile points". *Proceedings of the 6th Plains Conference for Archaeology (1948), Anthropological Papers, No. 11*, Department of Anthropology, University of Utah, Salt Lake City, pp. 117-124.

Krieger, Alex D. (Editor)
582. 1953 "Notes and News: Early Man". *American Antiquity*, Vol. 18, No. 3, pp. 289-291.

Krieger, Alex D.
583. 1954 "A comment on 'Fluted point relationships' by John Witthoft". *American Antiquity,* "Facts and Comments", *Vol. 19, No. 3, pp. 273-275.*

Krieger, Alex D. (Assembler)
584. 1956a "Early Man". *American Antiquity*, "Notes and News", Vol. 21, No. 4, pp. 449-452.

585. 1956b "Early Man". *American Antiquity*, "Notes and News", Vol. 22, No. 1, pp. 105-107.

Kreiger, Alex D.
586. 1962 Comments on, "The Paleo-Indian tradition in eastern North America", by Ronald J. Mason. In, *Current Anthropology*, Vol. 3, No. 3, Chicago, pp. 256-259.

587. 1963 Comments on, "The Upper Palaeolithic and the New World", by E.F. Greenman. In, *Current Anthropology*, Vol. 4, No. 1, pp. 74-76.

588. 1964 "Early Man in the New World". In, *Prehistoric man in the New World*, Jesse D. Jennings and Edward Norbeck, (Editors). The University of Chicago Press, Chicago, pp. 23-81.

Kruse, Harvey R.

589. 1939 "The significance of glacial Lake Agassiz to Minnesota archaeology". *Minnesota Archaeologist*, Vol. V, pp. 32-41.

590. 1941a "Another Yuma is found along the ancient migration route of northern Minnesota; Collection of Judge A.G.W. Anderson". *Minnesota Archaeologist*, Vol. 7, p. 21.

591. 1941b "Three new discoveries in America emphasize again the importance of this state's location along the probable migration route of ancient man". *Minnesota Archaeologist*, Vol. 7, pp. 52-54.

Kuhm, Herbert W.

592. 1934 "The Folsom point controversy". *Wisconsin Archeologist*, Vol. 14, No. 2, pp. 27-30.

Kümmel, Henry B.

593. 1898 "The age of the artifact-bearing sand at Trenton". *Proceedings of the American Association for the Advancement of Science*, 1897, Vol. 46, pp. 348-350.

Lance, John F.

594. 1955 "Problems in dating Early Man in North America by paleontology". *Plateau*, Vol. 27, No. 4, pp. 1-5.

Landis, H.K.

595. 1935 "Mammoths on gorgets". *Pennsylvania Archaeologist*, Vol. 5, No. 3, pp. 72-74.

Lang, Richard W.

596. 1962 "Preliminary cultural developmental interpretations of the lower central Allegheny Valley". *Archeological Newsletter*, No. 23, Section of Man, Carnegie Museum, Pittsburgh, pp. 7-10.

Laubach, Charles

597. 1893 "A few interesting finds in the Columbian gravels". *The Archaeologist*, Vol. 1, pp. 128-129.

Leary, Richard

598. 1968 "Mammoths and mastodons". *The Living Museum*, Vol. 30, No. 2, pp. 12-14.

Le Bounty, Larry W.

599. 1969 "A fluted point from Ashtabula County". *Ohio Archaeologist*, Vol. 19, No. 3, pp. 88-89.

Lee, Thomas E.

600. 1953 "A preliminary report on the Sheguiandah Site, Manitoulin Island". *Annual Report of the National Museum of Canada, 1951-52,* Bulletin 128, Ottawa, pp. 58-67.

601. 1954 "The first Sheguiandah expedition, Manitoulin Island, Ontario". *American Antiquity,* Vol. 20, No. 2, pp. 101-111.

602. 1955 "The second Sheguiandah expedition, Manitoulin Island, Ontario". *American Antiquity,* Vol. 21, No. 1, pp. 63-71.

603. 1956 "Position and meaning of a radio-carbon sample from the Sheguiandah Site, Ontario". *American Antiquity,* "Facts and Comments", Vol. 22, No. 1, p. 79.

604. 1957 "The antiquity of the Sheguiandah Site". *The Canadian Field-Naturalist,* Vol. 71, No. 3, pp. 117-137.

605. 1961 "A new hypothesis: The question of Indian origins". *Science of Man,* National Association of Local Anthropology Clubs, California, Vol. 1, No. 5, pp. 159-160, 165-167.

606. 1962 "The prehistory of Manitoulin Island, Ontario". *New World Antiquity,* Vol. 9, No. 8/9, pp. 101-122.

607. 1963a "Some comments on the Brohm Site of northern Ontario". *New World Antiquity,* Vol. 10, No. 1/2, pp. 11-18.

608. 1963b "Sheguiandah: A Point Peninsula workshop?" *New World Antiquity,* Vol. 10, No. 9/10, pp. 102-109.

609. 1964 "Sheguiandah: Workshop or habitation?" *Anthropological Journal of Canada,* Vol. 2, No. 3, pp. 16-24.

610. 1965a "A small cache of early points, Lac St-Jean, Quebec." *Anthropological Journal of Canada,* Vol. 3, No. 1, pp. 22-24.

611. 1965b "An unfluted Cumberland (Beaver Lake) point". *Anthropological Journal of Canada,* Vol. 3, No. 3, p. 38.

612. 1965c "A Point Peninsula Site, Manitoulin Island, Lake Huron". *Massachusetts Archaeological Society, Bulletin,* Vol. 26, No. 2, pp. 19-30.

613. 1968 "The question of Indian origins, again". *Anthropological Journal of Canada,* Vol. 6, No. 4, pp. 22-32.

614. 1971 "Some Comments on the Brohm Site of northern Ontario". *Anthropological Journal of Canada,* Vol. 9, No. 3, pp. 14-18.

615. 1972a "Sheguiandah in retrospect". *Anthropological Journal of Canada*, Vol. 10, No. 1, pp. 28-30. Also, Michigan Geological Survey, 1968.

616. 1972b "National Museum phantasies". *Anthropological Journal of Canada*, Vol. 11, No. 1, p. 26.

Leidy, Joseph
617. 1889 "Notice of some fossil human bones". *Transactions of the Wagner Free Institute of Science*, Vol. 2, pp. 9-12.

Leighton, Morris M.
618. 1933 "Some observations on the antiquity of man in Illinois". *Transactions of the Illinois State Academy of Science*, Vol. 25, p. 83.

Leslie, Vernon E.
619. 1958 "Arrowpoint classification—again". *Pennsylvania Archaeologist*, Vol. 28, No. 2, pp. 77-82.

620. 1964 "The Palaeo and the Archaic in the upper Delaware Valley". *Chesopiean*, Vol. 2, No. 4, pp. 69-85. Revised from an earlier version and published in *New World Antiquity*, Vol. 10, Nos. 3/4, 1963.

Leverett, Frank
621. 1892 "Relation of a Loveland, Ohio, implement-bearing terrace to the moraines of the ice sheet". *Proceedings of the American Association for the Advancement of Science*, 1891, Vol. 40, pp. 361-362.

622. 1893 "Supposed glacial man in southwestern Ohio". *American Geologist*, Vol. 11, pp. 186-189.

623. 1931 "The Pensacola terrace and associated beaches and bars in Florida". *Florida State Geological Survey, Bulletin* No. 7, pp. 33-37.

Lewis, Clifford M.
624. 1958 "Fluted and other early hunter points from West Virginia". *West Virginia Archeologist*, No. 10, pp. 10-12.

Lewis, Henry Carvill
625. 1880 "The Trenton gravel and its relation to the antiquity of man". *Proceedings of the Academy of Natural Science*, Philadelphia, pp. 296-309.

626. 1881a "The antiquity and origin of the Trenton gravel". In, *Primitive industry or illustrations of the handiwork in stone, bone and clay, of the native races of the northern Atlantic seaboard of America*, by Charles C. Abbott, M.D. George A. Bates, Salem Massachusetts, pp. 523-551.

627. 1881b "The antiquity of man in eastern America, geologically considered". Abstract, *Proceedings of the American Association for the Advancement of Science*, Vol. 29, pp. 706-709.

628. 1883 "On a supposed human implement from the gravel at Philadelphia". *Proceedings of the Academy of Natural Sciences of Philadelphia*.

Lewis, Thomas M.N.

629. 1947 "Mastodon points from southwest Virginia". *Tennessee Archaeologist*, Vol. 4, No. 3, p. 22.

630. 1950 "Folsom flakes". *Tennessee Archaeologist*, Vol. 6, No. 1, p. 6.

631. 1951 "Fluted points". *Tennessee Archaeologist*, Vol. 7, No. 2, pp. 59-60.

632. 1952 "Eastern fluted points". *Tennessee Archaeologist*, Vol. 8, No. 2, p. 57.

633. 1953a "The Paleo-Indian problem in Tennessee". *Tennessee Archaeologist*, Vol. 9, No. 2, pp. 38-40.

634. 1953b "A 'Trowel' and Clovis point from Bedford County". *Tennessee Archaeologist*, Vol. 9, No. 2, pp. 46-47.

635. 1954a "Early projectile points from Bedford County". *Tennessee Archaeologist*, Vol. 10, No. 1, pp. 21-23.

636. 1954b "Sandia points". *Tennessee Archaeologist*, Vol. 10, No. 1, pp. 26-27.

637. 1954c "Paleo points". *Tennessee Archaeologist*, Vol. 10, No. 1, p. 32.

638. 1954d "A suggested basis for Paleo-Indian chronology in Tennessee and the eastern United States". *Southern Indian Studies*, Vol. 5, No. 6-7, pp. 11-13.

639. 1954e "The Cumberland point". *Oklahoma Anthropological Society, Bulletin*, Vol. 2, pp. 7-8.

Lewis, Thomas M.N., and Madeline Kneberg

640. 1951 "Early projectile point forms, and examples from Tennessee". *Tennessee Archaeologist*, Vol. 7, No. 1, pp. 6-19.

641. 1955a "Cumberland point". *Tennessee Archaeologist*, Vol. 11, No. 1, p. 31.

642. 1955b "Clovis point from Bledsoe County". *Tennessee Archaeologist*, Vol. 11, No. 1, p. 32.

643. 1955c "Further evidence of Paleo-Indian occupation in Sumner and Trousdale Counties, Tennessee". *Tennessee Archaeologist*, Vol. 11, No. 1, pp. 33-34.

644. 1955d "Paleo-Indian point from Meigs County". *Tennessee Archaeologist*, Vol. 11, No. 1, pp. 35-36.

645. 1955e "The A.L. Le Croy Collection". *Tennessee Archaeologist*, Vol. 11, No. 2, pp. 75-82.

646. 1955f "The Frank Parker Collection". *Tennessee Archaeologist*, Vol. 11, No. 2, pp. 82-83.

647. 1955g "A reworked Clovis point". *Tennessee Archaeologist*, Vol. 11, No. 2, pp. 84-85.

648. 1955h "Early man site in Transylvania County, North Carolina". *Tennessee Archaeologist*, Vol. 11, No. 2, pp. 87-88.

649. 1955i "A Clovis point from vicinity of Knoxville". *Tennessee Archaeologist*, Vol. 11, No. 2, p. 90.

650. 1955j "Some early Tennessee projectile points". *Tennessee Archaeologist*, Vol. 11, No. 2, pp. 90-91.

651. 1956a "The Paleo-Indian complex on the LeCroy Site". *Tennessee Archaeologist*, Vol. 12, No. 1, pp. 5-12.

652. 1956b "Specimens from the Pitts Collection". *Tennessee Archaeologist*, Vol. 12, No. 1, pp. 32-35.

653. 1956c "A point with oblique parallel flaking". *Tennessee Archaeologist*, Vol. 12, No. 1, p. 35.

654. 1956d "Fluted points from Chickamauga Lake area". *Tennessee Archaeologist*, Vol. 12, No. 1, p. 36.

655. 1956e "Smith County Cumberland points". *Tennessee Archaeologist*, Vol. 12, No. 2, p. 43.

656. 1956f "Fluted points from Kentucky Lake region". *Tennessee Archaeologist*, Vol. 12, No. 2, p. 44.

657. 1957a "The Camp Creek Site". *Tennessee Archaeologist*, Vol. 13, No. 1, pp. 1-48.

658. 1957b "Paleo points from a Kentucky Lake site". *Tennessee Archaeologist*, Vol. 13, No. 1, p. 74.

659. 1957c "Kentucky Lake points". *Tennessee Archaeologist*, Vol. 13, No. 2, p. 98.

660. 1958a "Fine Clovis point from Shelby County". *Tennessee Archaeologist*, Vol. 14, No. 1, pp. 34-35.

661. 1958b "Early types of projectile points from Benton County, Tennessee". *Tennessee Archaeologist*, Vol. 14, No. 1, pp. 36-37.

662. 1958c "The Nuckolls Site". *Tennessee Archaeologist*, Vol. 14, No. 2, pp. 60-79.

663. 1958d "Cumberland points from Overton County". *Tennessee Archaeologist*, Vol. 14, No. 2, p. 95.

664. 1958e "Hiwassee River Paleo points". *Tennessee Archaeologist*, Vol. 14, No. 2, p. 97.

665. 1958f "Along the Mississippi in Tennessee". *Tennessee Archaeologist*, Vol. 14, No. 2, pp. 97-99.

666. 1958g *Tribes that slumber, Indians of the Tennessee region.* University of Tennessee Press, Knoxville, 196 pp.

667. 1959a "Early points from Stewart County, Tennessee". *Tennessee Archaeologist*, Vol. 15, No. 1, pp. 60-61.

668. 1959b "A Bedford County site". *Tennessee Archaeologist*, Vol. 15, No. 1, p. 61.

669. 1959c "Paleo points from Bedford County, Tennessee". *Tennessee Archaeologist*, Vol. 15, No. 1, pp. 63-64.

670. 1959d "Clovis point from Giles County, Tennessee". *Tennessee Archaeologist*, Vol. 15, No. 1, p. 64.

671. 1959e "Dale Hollow Lake specimens". *Tennessee Archaeologist*, Vol. 15, No. 1, p. 65.

672. 1959f "David C. Hulse Collection". *Tennessee Archaeologist*, Vol. 15, No. 2, pp. 121-126.

673. 1959g "Additional Nuckolls' Site material". *Tennessee Archaeologist*, Vol. 15, No. 2, pp. 127-132.

674. 1959h "Aaron B. Clements Collection". *Tennessee Archaeologist*, Vol. 15, No. 2, pp. 133-141.

675. 1959i "Three Paleo points from Kentucky Lake area". *Tennessee Archaeologist*, Vol. 15, No. 2, pp. 142-143.

676. 1959j "Meigs County artifacts". *Tennessee Archaeologist*, Vol. 15, No. 2, p. 143.

677. 1960a "J.A. Schuler Collection". *Tennessee Archaeologist*, Vol. 16, No. 1, pp. 30-34.

678. 1960b "Early artifacts from Hamilton County". *Tennessee Archaeologist*, Vol. 16, No. 1, pp. 35-36.

679. 1960c "Burbage Collection". *Tennessee Archaeologist*, Vol. 16, No. 1, pp. 36-39.

680. 1960d "The Pickett Site". *Tennessee Archaeologist*, Vol. 16, No. 1, pp. 46-48.

681. 1960e "Aaron B. Clement Collection". *Tennessee Archaeologist*, Vol. 16, No. 1, pp. 49-53.

682. 1960f "The Guinn Collection". *Tennessee Archaeologist*, Vol. 16, No. No. 1, pp. 54-61.

683. 1960g "The Guntersville, Alabama area". *Tennessee Archaeologist*, Vol. 16, No. 2, pp. 108-125.

684. 1960h "Cumberland point". *Tennessee Archaeologist*, Vol. 16, No. 2, p. 125.

685. 1960i "Paleo-Indian artifacts in Burbage Collection". *Tennessee Archaeologist*, Vol. 16, No. 2, pp. 126-127.

Little, Glade
686. 1960 "A fluted point from Putnam County, W. Va." *The West Virginia Archeologist*, No. 12, pp. 22-23.

Lively, Matthew
687. 1965a *The Lively Complex.* Alabama Archaeological Society, Birmingham, Alabama.

688. 1965b "The Lively Complex: Announcing a pebble tool industry in Alabama". *Journal of Alabama Archaeology*, Vol. 11, No. 2, pp. 103-122.

Lively, Matthew, A.G. Long, Jr., and Daniel W. Josselyn
689. 1965 "A preliminary report and technological discussion of the Lively Complex of pebble tools in Alabama". Privately published, Josselyn, Birmingham.

Long, Russell J.

690. 1953 "Glacial drift artifacts". *Ohio Archaeologist,* Vol. 3, No. 4, pp. 24-25.

691. 1967 "The Tom Brown Folsom". *Ohio Archaeologist,* Vol. 17, pp. 12-13.

Loomis, F.B.

692. 1924 "Artifacts associated with the remains of a Columbian elephant at Melbourne, Florida". *American Journal of Science,* Fifth Series, Vol. VIII, (Whole Number *CCVIII*), No. 48, pp. 503-508.

693. 1925 "The Florida man". *Science,* N.S., Vol. 62, p. 436.

694. 1926 "Early Man in Florida". *Natural History,* Vol. 26, No. 3, pp. 260-262.

Lowther, Gordon

695. 1955 "Archeology in the province of Quebec". In, *A survey of the aboriginal populations of Quebec and Labrador,* Jacob Fried (Editor), Eastern Canadian Anthropological Series, No. 1, McGill University, Montreal, Quebec, pp. 65-73.

Lubbock, Sir John

696. 1863 "North American archaeology". *Smithsonian Institution, Annual Report, 1862,* pp. 318-336.

697. 1878 *Pre-historic times; as illustrated by ancient remains, and the manners and customs of modern savages.* Fourth Edition, D. Appleton and Company, Broadway, New York, 655 pp.

Lyell, Charles

698. 1844 "On the geological position of the *mastodon giganteum* and associated fossil remains at Bigbone Lick, Kentucky, and other localities in the United States and Canada". *American Journal of Science and Arts,* Vol. 46, pp. 320-323.

MacCord, Howard A.

699. 1964 "Late Pleistocene remains found in Virginia". *Archeological Society of Virginia, Quarterly Bulletin,* Vol. 18, No. 3, pp. 61-62.

McCurdy, George Grant

700. 1914 "The passing of a Connecticut rockshelter". *American Journal of Science,* Fourth Series, Vol. *XXXVIII,* (Whole Number *CLXXXVIII*), No. 228, pp. 511-522.

701. 1917a "Archaeological evidences of man's antiquity at Vero, Florida". *Journal of Geology,* Vol. 25, No. 1, pp. 56-62.

702. 1917b "The problem of man's antiquity at Vero, Florida". *American Anthropologist*, N.S., Vol. 19, pp. 252-261.

McCurdy, George Grant (Editor)
703. 1937 *Early Man*: As depicted by leading authorities at the International Symposium, The Academy of Natural Sciences, Philadelphia, March, 1937. With Introduction by John C. Merriam. J.B. Lippincott Company, London, 362 pp.

MacDonald, George F.
704. 1966 "The technology and settlement pattern of a Paleo-Indian site at Debert, Nova Scotia". *Tirage a part de Quaternaria, VIII*, Roma.

705. 1967 Review of, "The Paleo-Indian occupation of the Holcombe Beach", by James E. Fitting, Jerry DeVisscher, and Edward J. Wahla. In, *American Antiquity*, Vol. 32, No. 3, pp. 407-408.

706. 1968 "Debert: A Palaeo-Indian site in central Nova Scotia". *Anthropology Papers*, No. 16, *National Museum of Canada*, Ottawa, 207 pp.

707. 1970 "A review of research on Paleo-Indian in eastern North America 1960-1970". Paper presented at American Anthropological Association meetings in San Diego, California.

708. 1971 "A review of research on Paleo-Indian in eastern North America, 1960-1970". In, Papers from a Symposium on Early Man in North America, New Developments: 1960-1970, held at the American Anthropological Association Meetings, San Diego, California, November 18-22, 1970. *Arctic Anthropology*, Vol. VIII, No. 2, pp. 32-41.

MacGowan, Ernest S.
709. 1945 "Making chipped artifacts from glacial pebbles". *Minnesota Archaeologist*, Vol. 11, pp. 18-21.

MacGowan, Kenneth
710. 1950 *Early Man in the New World.* Macmillan Company, New York.

MacGowan, Kenneth and Joseph A. Hester, Jr.
711. 1962 *Early Man in the New World.* Revised Edition, American Museum of Natural History, The Natural History Library, Anchor Books, Doubleday and Company, Incorporated, Garden City, New York, 333 pp.

MacLean, J.P.
712. 1875 "A manual of the anitquity of man". Published for the author, New York, pp. 114-122.

MacNeish, Richard S.

713. 1952a "The archeology of the northeastern United States". In, *Archeology of eastern United States*, James B. Griffin (Editor), University of Chicago Press, Chicago, pp. 46-58.

714. 1952b "A possible early site in the Thunder Bay District, Ontario". *The National Museum of Canada, Bulletin* 126, Ottawa, pp. 23-47.

Mahan, Edward C.

715. 1954 "A survey of Paleo-Indian & other early flint artifacts from sites in northern, western, & central Alabama—Part *I*". *Tennessee Archaeologist*, Vol. 10, pp. 37-58; Part *II*, Vol. 11, No. 1, pp. 1-7; Part *III*, Vol. 11, No. 2, pp. 68-70.

716. 1956 "A survey of Paleo, American and other early flint artifacts from Alabama—Part *IV*". *Tennessee Archaeologist*, Vol. 12, No. 1, pp. 12-14; Part *V*. "A Clovis camp site on Moses Hill, Mississippi", *ibid*, Vol. 12, No. 2, pp. 28-31.

717. 1968 "Traces of Early Man in north Alabama Paleo points from Raby's Trout Farm, Limestone County". *Journal of Alabama Archaeology*, "Facts and Comments", Vol. 14, No. 2, pp. 70-73.

718. 1969 "Early artifacts of candy stripe flint". *Journal of Alabama Archaeology*, "Facts and Comments", Vol. 15, No. 2, pp. 63-66.

719. 1970 "Lively complex traits on chalcedony nodules—Huntsville area, Alabama". *Tennessee Archaeologist*, Vol. 25, No. 2, pp. 47-58.

Manley, Frank

720. 1968a "Horseleg Mountain: A transitional Paleo-Indian site". *Archaeology*, Vol. 21, No. 1, pp. 54-60.

721. 1968b "Hills, bluffs and a Georgia Clovis point". *Archaeology*, "Archaeological News", Vol. 21, No. 2, pp. 138-139.

Markley, Max C.

722. 1939 "Folsom and Yuma points in Minnesota". *Minnesota Archaeologist*, Vol. 5, pp. 42-45.

Martijn, Charles A.

723. 1969a "Late-Pleistocene and post-glacial ecological sequence in south and central Quebec, Canada: A preliminary discussion". In, "Mistasini-Albanel, contributions to the prehistory of Quebec", by Charles A. Martijn, and Edward S. Rogers. *Travaux Divers*, No. 25, *Centre d'Études Nordiques*, Université Laval, Québec, pp. 25-67.

724. 1969b "Prehistoric cultural developments in central Quebec, Canada: A provisional interpretation". In, "Mistassini-Albanel, contributions to

the prehistory of Quebec", by Charles A. Martijn, and Edward S. Rogers. *Travaux Divers*, No. 25, *Centre d'Études Nordiques*, Université Laval, Québec, pp. 309-378.

Martijn, Charles A., and Edward S. Rogers
725.   1969   "Mistassini-Albanel, contributions to the prehistory of Quebec". *Travaux Divers*, No. 25, *Centre d'Etudes Nordiques*, Université Laval, Québec.

Martijn, Charles A., and Richard E. Morlan
726.   1966   "Twenty projectile points and knives from central Quebec, Canada". *Le Bulletin de la Société D'Archéologie de Québec*, parait 4 sois l'an, Décembre, pp. 15-30.

Martin, Paul S.
727.   1958   "Taiga-tundra and the full-glacial period in Chester County, Pennsylvania". *American Journal of Science*, Vol. 256, pp. 470-502.

728.   1967   "Prehistoric overkill". In, *Pleistocene extinctions: The search for a cause*, P.S. Martin and H.E. Wright, Jr. (Editors). Volume 6 of the Proceedings of the *VIIth* Congress of the International Association for Quaternary Research. Yale University Press, New Haven and London, pp. 75-120.

729.   1970   "Pleistocene niches for alien animals". *BioScience*, Vol. 20, No. 4, pp. 218-221.

730.   1973   "The discovery of America". *Science*, Vol. 179, No. 4077, pp. 969-974.

Martin, Paul S., George Irving Quimby, and Donald Collier
731.   1947   *Indians before Columbus: Twenty thousand years of North American history revealed by archeology.* University of Chicago Press, Chicago.

Mason, Ronald J.
732.   1956   "A fluted point from Bucks County, Pennsylvania". *Pennsylvania Archaeologist*, Vol. 26, No. 1, pp. 3-4.

733.   1957   "Additional fluted point data from southeastern Pennsylvania". *Pennsylvania Archaeologist*, Vol. 27, No. 1, pp. 39-42.

734.   1958a   "Fluted point measurements". *American Antiquity*, Vol. 23, No. 3, pp. 311-312.

735.   1958b   "Late Pleistocene geochronology and the Paleo-Indian penetration into the lower Michigan Peninsula". *Anthropological Papers*, No. 11, *Museum of Anthropology*, University of Michigan, Ann Arbor, 48 pp.

736. 1958c "Time-depth and Early Man in the Delaware Valley". *Archaeological Society of Delaware, Bulletin* 9, No. 1, Claymont, pp. 1-10.

737. 1959 "Indications of Paleo-Indian occupation in the Delaware Valley". *Pennsylvania Archaeologist*, Vol. 29, No. 1, pp. 1-17.

738. 1960 "Early Man and the age of the Champlain Sea". *Journal of Geology*, Vol. 68, No. 4, pp. 366-376.

739. 1962 "The Paleo-Indian tradition in eastern North America". *Current Anthropology*, Vol. 3, No. 3, pp. 227-246, "Reply" pp. 271-274.

740. 1963 "Two late Paleo-Indian complexes in Wisconsin". *Wisconsin Archeologist*, Vol. 44, No. 4, pp. 199-211.

741. 1967 Review of, *Late Paleo and early Archaic manifestations in western Kentucky*, by Martha A. Rolingson and Douglas W. Schwartz. In, *American Anthropologist*, Vol. 69, No. 1, pp. 102-103.

Mason, Ronald J., and Carol Irwin

742. 1960 "An Eden-Scottsbluff burial in northeastern Wisconsin". *American Antiquity*, Vol. 26, No. 1, pp. 43-57.

Matson, Frederick, R.

743. 1955 "Charcoal concentration from early sites for radiocarbon dating". *American Antiquity*, Vol. 21, pp. 162-169.

Matsumoto, H.

744. 1918 "On the fossil human bones found at Vero, Florida", *Anthropological Society of Tokyo, Journal*, Vol. 33, No. 374. Text in Japanese.

Matthew, G.F.

745. 1884 "Discoveries at a village of the Stone Age at Bocabec N.B." *Natural History Society of New Brunswick, Bulletin* No. 3, pp. 6-29.

Maxwell, Moreau S.

746. 1952 "The archeology of the lower Ohio Valley". In, *Archeology of eastern United States*, James B. Griffin (Editor), The University of Chicago Press, Chicago, pp. 176-187.

Mayer-Oakes, William J.

747. 1951 "Archeological problems in the upper Ohio Valley. Part 1—The southern area". *Pennsylvania Archaeologist*, Vol. 21, Nos. 3-4, pp. 53-56.

748. 1952 "Archeological problems in the upper Ohio Valley. Part 2—The northern area". *Pennsylvania Archaeologist*, Vol. 22, No. 1, pp. 37-40.

749. 1953 "Archeological problems in the upper Ohio Valley. Part 3—The central area". *Pennsylvania Archaeologist*, Vol. 23, No. 2, pp. 64-67.

750. 1955a "Prehistory of the upper Ohio Valley; An introductory archaeological study". *Annals of the Carnegie Museum* 34, Anthropological Series No. 2, Pittsburgh, 296 pp.

751. 1959 "Relationship between Plains early hunter and eastern Archaic". *Journal of Washington Academy of Science*, Vol. 49, No. 5, pp. 146-156.

752. 1970 "Archeological investigations in the Grand Rapids, Manitoba, reservoir, 1961-1962". *Occasional Papers, No. 3, Department of Anthropology, University of Manitoba.*

McAvoy, Joseph M.

753. 1965 "An early chert assemblage in Chesterfield County, Virginia". *Archeological Society of Virginia, Quarterly Bulletin*, Vol. 20, No. 2, pp. 48-50.

754. 1967a "Distinctive lithic materials preferred by Early Man in Virginia for production of chipped tools and projectile points. Part I—Large grain quartzite". *The Chesopiean*, Vol. 5, No. 3, pp. 61-63.

755. 1967b "The J.G. Pritchard Clovis". *The Chesopiean*, Vol. 5, Nos. 5 and 6, pp. 136-137.

McCary, Ben C.

756. 1946 "A report on Folsom-like points found in Granville County, North Carolina". *Archeological Society of Virginia, Quarterly Bulletin*, Vol. 3, No. 1, pp. 3-14.

757. 1947a "Folsom points". *Archeological Society of Virginia, Quarterly Bulletin*, Vol. 1, No. 3.

758. 1947b "A survey and study of Folsom-like points found in Virginia". *Archeological Society of Virginia, Quarterly Bulletin*, Vol. 2, No. 1.

759. 1947c "A report of additional Virginia Folsom points". *Archeological Society of Virginia, Quarterly Bulletin*, Vol. 2, No. 2.

760. 1948a "Report of additional Virginia—Folsom points numbers 137-141". *Archeological Society of Virginia, Quarterly Bulletin*, Vol. 2, No. 3.

761. 1948b "A report on Folsom-like points found in Granville County, North Carolina". *Archeological Society of Virginia, Quarterly Bulletin*, Vol. 3, No. 1.

762. 1948c "The Folsom-like points of Virginia". *The Commonwealth*, Vol. 15, No. 2.

763. 1949a "Projectile forms from Indian sites in Albemarle County, Va." *Archeological Society of Virginia, Quarterly Bulletin*, Vol. 3, No. 3.

764. 1949b "Survey of Virginia-Folsom points 142-161". *Archeological Society of Virginia, Quarterly Bulletin*, Vol. 4, No. 1.

765. 1949c "A Folsom workshop site on the Williamson Farm, Dinwiddie County". *Archeological Society of Virginia, Quarterly Bulletin*, Vol. 4, No. 2.

766. 1951a "A workshop site of Early Man in Dinwiddie County, Virginia". *American Antiquity*, Vol. 17, No. 1, pp. 9-17.

767. 1951b "The Johnson Mill rock-shelter, Albemarle County, Va." *Archeological Society of Virginia, Quarterly Bulletin*, Vol. 6, No. 1.

768. 1952 "Survey of Virginia-Folsom points 173-219". *Archeological Society of Virginia, Quarterly Bulletin*, Vol. 6, No. 4.

769. 1953a "A Paleo-Indian workshop site in Dinwiddie County, Virginia". *Eastern States Archeological Federation, Bulletin* No. 12, pp. 6-7

770. 1953b "Survey of Virginia fluted points nos. 220-225". *Archeological Society of Virginia, Quarterly Bulletin*, Vol. 7, No. 3.

771. 1953c "A Virginia fluted point". *Archeological Society of Virginia, Quarterly Bulletin*, Vol. 8, No. 1, p. 16.

772. 1954a "A Paleo-Indian workshop in Dinwiddie County, Virginia". *Southern Indian Studies*, Vol. 5, pp. 9-10.

773. 1954b "Survey of Virginia fluted points, nos. 226-231". *Archeological Society of Virginia, Quarterly Bulletin*, Vol. 8, No. 3, pp. 14-16.

774. 1956a "Survey of Virginia fluted points, Nos., 232-263". *Archeological Society of Virginia, Quarterly Bulletin*, Vol. 10, No. 3, pp. 10-16.

775. 1956b "A fluted point from Rockbridge County, Virginia". *Archeological Society of Virginia, Quarterly Bulletin*, Vol. 10, No. 4, pp. 14-16

776. 1958 "Survey of Virginia fluted points, Nos. 265-281". *Archeological Society of Virginia, Quarterly Bulletin*, Vol. 13, No. 1, pp. 3-7.

777. 1961 "Survey of Virginia fluted points; Numbers 282-293". *Archeological Society of Virginia, Quarterly Bulletin*, Vol. 15, No. 3, pp. 27-31.

778. 1963a "Archeology of the western area of Dismal Swamp". *Eastern States Archeological Federation, Bulletin* No. 22, pp. 11-12.

779. 1963b "Survey of Virginia fluted points, Numbers 294-314". *Archeological Society of Virginia, Quarterly Bulletin*, Vol. 18, No. 2, pp. 25-29.

780. 1965 "Survey of Virginia fluted points, Numbers 315-347". *Archeological Society of Virginia, Quarterly Bulletin*, Vol. 20, No. 2, pp. 53-60.

781. 1968 "Survey of Virginia fluted points, nos. 348-384". *Archeological Society of Virginia, Quarterly Bulletin*, Vol. 23, No. 1, pp. 2-10.

782. 1972 "Survey of Virginia fluted points, nos. 385-420". *Archeological Society of Virginia, Quarterly Bulletin*, Vol. 26, No. 4, pp. 190-202.

McCary, Ben C., J.C. Smith, and C.E. Gilliam
783. 1949 "A Folsom workshop site on the Williamson Farm, Dinwiddie County, Virginia". *Archeological Society of Virginia, Quarterly Bulletin*, Vol 4, No. 2.

McGee, W.J.
784. 1888 "Paleolithic man in America: His antiquity and his environment". *Popular Science Monthly*, Vol. 34, pp. 20-36.

785. 1889 "The geologic antecedents of man in the Potomac Valley". *American Anthropologist*, Vol. 2, pp. 227-234.

786. 1893 "Man and the glacial period". *American Anthropologist*, Vol. 6, pp. 85-95.

McMichael, Edward V.
787. 1962 "Archeological problems in central west Virginia". *Eastern States Archeological Federation, Bulletin* No. 21, p. 14.

Mercer, Henry C.
788. 1885 *The Lenape stone, or the Indian and the mammoth.* New York. Publisher unknown.

789. 1893a "Trenton and Somme gravel specimens compared with ancient quarry refuse in America and Europe". Reprint from the *American Naturalist*, 16 pp. pamphlet.

790. 1893b "Discovery of ancient argillite quarries on the Delaware". *The Archaeologist*, Vol. 1, pp. 172-174.

791. 1893c "Pebbles chipped by modern Indians as an aid to the study of the Trenton gravel implements". *Proceedings of the American Associa- Association for the Advancement of Science,* Vol. 41, 1892, pp. 287-289.

792. 1896 "Cave exploration in the eastern United States: Preliminary report". *Leaflets* in *Department of American and Prehistoric Archaeology*, University of Pennsylvania, June 4.

793. 1897 "Researches upon the antiquity of man in the Delaware Valley and the eastern United States". *Publications of the University of Pennsylvania, Series of Philology, Literature and Archaeology*, Vol. 6, Boston.

794. 1898 "A new investigation of man's antiquity at Trenton". *Proceedings of the American Association for the Advancement of Science* 1897, Vol. 46, pp. 370-378.

Merriam, John C.

795. 1933 "Present status of the problem of the antiquity of man in North America". Abstract, *Science*, N.S., Vol. 78, No. 2032, p. 524.

796. 1935 "A review of evidence relating to the status of the problem of antiquity of man in Florida". *Science*, N.S., Vol. 82, No. 2118, p. 103.

797. 1936 "Present status of knowledge relating to antiquity of man in America". *16th International Geological Congress Report*, Vol. 2, Washington, pp. 1313-1323.

798. 1937 "Introductory remarks". In, *Early Man:* As depicted by leading authorities at the International Symposium, The Academy of Natural Sciences, Philadelphia, March, 1937, George Grant MacCurdy (Editor). J.B. Lippincott Company, London, pp. 19-22.

Michels, J.W.

799. 1967 "Report on radiocarbon dated samples from Sheep rock shelter". In, *Archaeological Investigations of Sheep rock shelter*, J.W. Michels and I.F. Smith (Editors). The Pennsylvania State University, Department of Anthropology, University Park, p. 863.

Michener, Carolee K.

800. 1954 "Archaeological sites of Venango County". *Pennsylvania Archaeologist*, Vol. 24, Nos. 3-4, pp. 127-134.

Michie, James L.

801. 1967a "South Carolina Dalton points and their variations". *The Chesopiean*, Vol. 5, No. 1, pp. 15-18.

802. 1967b "Fluted points of South Carolina coast". *The Chesopiean*, Vol. 5, No. 2, pp. 54-56.

803. 1971 "The Taylor Site: An early Archaic-Paleo Indian site". Abstract of a paper given at the 1970 annual meeting of the Eastern States Archeological Federation. *Eastern States Archeological Federation, Bulletin* No. 30, pp. 14-15.

Miller, Carl Frederick

804. 1948 "Early cultural manifestations exposed by the archaeological survey of Buggs Island reservoir in southern Virginia and northern North Carolina". *Journal of Washington Academy of Science*, Vol. 38, No. 12, pp. 397-399.

805. 1950 "Early cultural horizons in the southeastern United States". *American Antiquity*, Vol. 15, No. 4, pp. 273-288.

806. 1956a "Burin types from southern Virginia; a preliminary statement". *American Antiquity*, Vol. 21, p. 311.

807. 1956b "Life 8,000 years ago uncovered in an Alabama cave". *The National Geographic Magazine*, Vol. 110, No. 4, pp. 542-558.

808. 1957 "Radiocarbon dates from an early Archaic deposit in Russell Cave, Alabama". *American Antiquity*, Vol. 23, No. 1, p. 84.

809. 1958 "Russell Cave: New light on Stone Age life". *The National Geographic Magazine*, Vol. 113, No. 3, pp. 426-437.

810. 1961 "Some unique bone tools from Russell Cave, northern Alabama". *Eastern States Archeological Federation Bulletin* No. 20, p. 15.

811. 1962a Comments on, "The Paleo-Indian tradition in eastern North America", by Ronald J. Mason. In, *Current Anthropology*, Vol. 3, No. 3, Chicago, p. 259.

812. 1962b "Archeology of the John H. Kerr reservoir basin, Roanoke River Virginia-North Carolina". *Bureau of American Ethnology, Bulletin 182, River Basin Survey Paper,* No. 25, Washington, D.C. pp. 1-327.

813. 1965 "Paleo-Indian and early Archaic projectile point forms from Russell Cave northern Alabama". *Anthropological Journal of Canada*, Vol. 3, No. 2, pp. 2-5.

814. 1972 "Russell Cave (Alabama) archeology". *National Geographic Society Research Reports 1955-1960*, National Geographic Society, Washington, D.C., pp. 115-121.

Mills, Richard S.

815. 1972 "Mice, men and mastadons". *The Explorer*, Vol. 14, No. 2, pp. 9-12.

Mills, W.C.

816. 1892 "Discovery of a Palaeolithic implement at New Comerstown, Ohio". Report by Mr. W.C. Mills and Prof. G. Frederick Wright. *Western Reserve Historical Society*, Vol. 3, No. 75, pp. 163-176.

Moffett, Ross

817.   1949   "The Raisch-Smith Site: An early Indian occupation in Preble County, Ohio". *Ohio State Archaeological and Historical Quarterly*, Vol. 58, pp. 428-441.

818.   1958   "A review of Cape Cod archaeology". *Massachusetts Archaeological Society, Bulletin* Vol. 19, No. 1, pp. 1-19.

Montagu, M.F. Ashley

819.   1955   "The Natchez innominate bone". *Human Biology*, Vol. 27, pp. 193-201.

Moorehead, Warren King

820.   1895   "A preliminary exploration of Ohio caves". *The Archaeologist*, Vol. III, No. 9, pp. 304-312, Official Organ of the Ohio State Archaeological and Historical Society, Columbus, Ohio.

821.   1900   *Prehistoric implements, a reference book.* Robert Clarke Company, Publishers, Cincinnati, Ohio.

Morgan, Richard G.

822.   1952   "Outline of cultures in the Ohio Region". In, *Archeology of eastern United States,* James B. Griffin (Editor), University of Chicago Press, Chicago, pp. 83-98.

Morse, Dan F.

823.   1971a   "Recent indications of Dalton settlement pattern in northeast Arkansas". Proceedings of the Twenty-Seventh Southeastern Archaeological Conference, Bulletin 13, pp. 5-10.

824.   1971b   "The Hawkins cache: A significant Dalton find in northeast Arkansas". *Arkansas Archeologist*, Vol. 12, No. 1, pp. 9-20.

825.   1973   "Dalton culture in northeast Arkansas". *The Florida Anthropologist*, Vol. 26, No. 1, pp. 23-38.

Morse, Dan F., Phyllis A. Morse, and John Waggoner, Jr.

826.   1964   "Fluted points from Smith County, Tennessee". *Tennessee Archaeologist*, Vol. 20, No. 1, pp. 16-34.

Mortine, Wayne A.

827.   1965   "Palaeo artifacts from the Newcomerstown area". *Ohio Archaeologist*, Vol. 15, No. 4, pp. 134-135.

828.   1968   "The Keiser Site: A Paleo-Indian site in Tuscarawas County". *Ohio Archaeologist*, Vol. 18, No. 1, pp. 12-16.

Mosely, S.A.

829.   1959   "The Nebo Hill Site—An Early Man site near Decatur, Alabama". *Journal of Alabama Archeology*, Vol. 5, No. 3, pp. 55-70.

Mounier, R. Alan
830. 1972 "The question of man's antiquity in the New World: 1840-1927". *Pennsylvania Archaeologist*, Vol. 42, No. 3, pp. 59-69.

Müller-Beck, Hansjürgen
831. 1962 Comments on, "The Paleo-Indian tradition in eastern North America", by Ronald J. Mason. In, *Current Anthropology*, Vol. 3, No. 3, Chicago, pp. 259-261.

832. 1966 "Paleohunters in America: Origins and diffusion". *Science*, Vol. 152, No. 3726, pp. 1191-1210.

833. 1967 "On migrations of hunters across the Bering Land Bridge in the Upper Pleistocene". In, *The Bering Land Bridge*, David M. Hopkins (Editor), Stanford University Press, Stanford, California, pp. 373-408.

Munson, Patrick J., and N.L. Downs
834. 1968 "A surface collection of Plano and Paleo-Indian projectile points from central Illinois". *The Missouri Archaeologist*, Vol. 30, pp. 122-131

Munson, Patrick J., and John C. Frye
835. 1965 "Artifact from deposits of mid-Wisconsin age in Illinois". *Science*, Vol. 150, No. 3704, pp. 1722-1723.

Munson, Patrick J., and Alan D. Harn
836. 1971 "An archaeological survey of the American Bottoms and Wood River terrace". *Illinois State Museum, Reports of Investigations*, No. 21, 123 pp.

Neill, Wilfred T.
837. 1957 "The rapid mineralization of organic remains in Florida, and its bearing on supposed Pleistocene records". *The Quarterly Journal of the Florida Academy of Sciences*, Vol. 20, No. 1, pp. 1-13.

838. 1958 "A stratified early site at Silver Springs, Florida". *Florida Anthropologist*, Vol. 11, pp. 33-48.

839. 1963 "Three new Florida projectile point types, believed early". *Florida Anthropologist*, Vol. XVI, No. 4, pp. 99-104.

840. 1964a "The association of Suwannee points and extinct animals in Florida". *Florida Anthropologist*, Vol. 17, No. 1, pp. 17-32.

841. 1964b "Trilisa Pond, an early site in Marion County, Florida". *Florida Anthropologist*, Vol. 17, No. 4, pp. 187-200.

842. 1966 "An Eden-like projectile point from South Carolina". *Florida Anthropologist*, Vol. 19, No. 4, pp. 143-144.

843. 1971 "A Florida Paleo-Indian implement of ground stone". *Florida Anthropologist,* Vol. 24, No. 2, pp. 61-70.

Neill, Wilfred T., and James C. McKay
844. 1968 "A supposed 'Florida Folsom' point: A reflutation". *Florida Anthropologist,* Vol. 21, No. 4, pp. 122-124.

Nelson, N.C.
845. 1918a "Additional studies in the Pleistocene at Vero, Florida". *Science,* N.S., Vol. 47, pp. 394-395.

846. 1918b "Chronology in Florida". *American Museum of Natural History, Anthropological Papers,* Vol. 22, Part 2, pp. 77-103.

847. 1918c "Review of the Ninth Annual Report of the Florida Geological Survey". *Science,* N.S., Vol. 47, pp. 394-395.

848. 1933 "The antiquity of man in America in the light of archaeology". In, *The American Aborigines, their origin and antiquity,* Diamond Jenness (Editor). Fifth Pacific Science Congress, Canada, University of Toronto Press, Toronto, pp. 85-130.

849. 1936 "The antiquity of man in America in the light of archeology". *Annual Report of the Smithsonian Institution for 1935,* pp. 471-506.

Nero, Robert W.
850. 1955 "Surface indications of a possible early Archaic camp-site in Wisconsin". *Wisconsin Archeologist,* Vol. 36, No. 4, pp. 128-146.

851. 1957 "A 'graver' site in Wisconsin". *American Antiquity,* Vol. 22, No. 3, pp. 300-304.

Nichols, George W.
852. 1970 "The reverse hinge fracture problem in fluted point manufacture". In, *Memoir* No. 8, *Missouri Archaeological Society,* December, pp. 1-9.

Norbeck, Edward
853. 1962 Comments on, "The Paleo-Indian tradition in eastern North America", by Ronald J. Mason. In, *Current Anthropology,* Vol. 3, No. 3, Chicago, p. 261.

Norick, Frank A.
854. 1962 "A Sandia Type *II* point from Geauga County, Ohio". *American Antiquity,* Vol. 28, No. 1, pp. 92-93.

Norris, Stanley E.
855. 1953 "Is there a case for Pleistocene man in Ohio?" *Ohio Archaeologist,* Vol. 3, No. 2, pp. 19-29.

Nuckolls, John B.
856. 1958 "Paleo and early chipped flint artifacts". *Tennessee Archaeologist*, Vol. 14, No. 1, pp. 24-25.

Olsen, Stanley J.
857. 1958 "The Wakulla Cave". *Natural History*, Vol. 67, No. 7, pp. 396-398, 401-403.

Omwake, H. Geiger
858. 1936 "Comment on Delaware Folsoms". *Archaeological Society of Delaware, Bulletin*, Vol. 2, No. 4, pp. 1-2.

Painter, Floyd E.
859. 1960 "A tidewater mastodon kill". *Archeological Society of Virginia, Quarterly Bulletin*, Vol. 15, No. 1, pp. 4-6.

860. 1964a "Paleo-Indian projectile points of Indiana". *Central States Archaeological Journal*, Vol. 2, No. 4, pp. 133-135.

861. 1964b "Paleo-Indian projectile points of Georgia". Abstract, *The Chesopiean*, Vol. 2, No. 3, pp. 46-48.

862. 1965a "The Cattail Creek fluting tradition". *The Chesopiean.* Vol. 3, No. 1, pp. 11-18.

863. 1965b "Paleo-Indian projectile points of Tennessee and Kentucky". *The Chesopiean*, Vol. 3, No. 3, pp. 72-75.

864. 1965c "Palaeo-Indian projectile points from Ohio". *Ohio Archaeologist*, Vol. 15, No. 2, pp. 67-69.

865. 1968 "Latest news on Early Man". *The Chesopiean*, Vol. 6, No. 4, pp. 83-86.

866. 1973 "The Cattail Creek fluting tradition and its complex-determining lithic debris". *Massachusetts Archaeological Society, Bulletin*, Vol. 34, Nos. 1-2, pp. 6-12.

Palmer, Kay L.
867. 1965 "'Pedigreed' fluted points". *Ohio Archaeologist*, Vol. 15, p. 30.

Parchert, Karl G.
868. 1944 "The Trenton Paleoliths". *The Totem Pole*, Vol. 13, No. 3, p. 3.

Parmalee, Paul W.
869. 1968 "Cave and archaeological faunal deposits as indicators of post-Pleistocene animal populations and distribution in Illinois". In, *The Quarternary of Illinois*, Robert E. Bergstrom (Editor), University of Illinois, College of Agriculture, Special Publication No. 14, Urbana, Illinois, pp. 104-113.

Paxton, C.L.

870. 1960 "Fluted and lanceolate points from the Kanawha Valley". *The West Virginia Archeologist*, No. 12, pp. 26-31.

Peabody, Charles

871. 1912a "L'homme fossile de Trenton (Etats-Unis)". *Congrès Préhistorique de France*, 7th, Nîmes., Compt Rendu, Paris, pp. 166-172.

872. 1912b "L'état présent de la question de l'homme glaciaire à Trenton, N.J.". *Congrès International d'Anthropologie et d'Archéologie Préhistoriques*, 14 session, Genève, t. 2, pp. 415-417.

Pease, A.P.L.

873. 1895 "Paleolithic implement found". *The Archaeologist*, Vol. 3, No. 2, pp. 74-75.

Peck, Rodney M.

874. 1969 "A Paleo-Indian camp site in Isle of Wight County, Virginia, (The Isle of Wight Site)". *The Chesopiean*, Vol. 7, No. 1, pp. 2-12.

Pendarvis, M.

875. 1953 "Evidence of Paleo-Indian culture in Sumner County". *Tennessee Archaeologist*, Vol. 9, No. 1, pp. 16-17.

Peru, Donald V.

876. 1965 "The distribution of fluted points in the counties of Kent and Allegan, Michigan". *Michigan Archaeologist*, Vol. 11, No. 1, pp. 1-8.

877. 1967 "The distribution of fluted points in Cass County, Michigan". *Michigan Archaeologist*, Vol. 13, No. 3, pp. 137-146.

878. 1969 "The Tolles Site". *Michigan Archaeologist*, Vol. 15, pp. 101-108.

Phelps, Mason M.

879. 1948 "Folsom-like points in Virginia". *Massachusetts Archaeological Society, Newsletter,* March, p. 2.

Pickle, R.W.

880. 1946 "Discovery of Folsom-like arrowpoint and artifacts of mastodon bone in southwest Virginia". *Tennessee Archaeologist*, Vol. 3, No. 1, pp. 3-7.

Pirsson, L.V.

881. 1911 Report on, "The Ice Age in North America and its bearings upon the antiquity of man", by G. Frederick Wright, Fifth Edition. In, *American Journal of Science*, Fourth Series, Vol. XXXII, (Whole Number CLXXXII), No. 187, pp. 70-71.

Pi-Sunyer, Oriol, John Edward Blank, and Robert Williams
882.   1967   "The Honey Run Site (33Co-3): A late Paleo-Indian locality in Coshocton County, Ohio". In, *Studies in Ohio Archaeology*, Olaf H. Prufer, and Douglas H. McKenzie (Editors), Western Reserve University Press, Cleveland, pp. 230-251.

Platcek, Eldon P.
883.   1965   "Preliminary survey of a Fowl Lakes site". *Minnesota Archaeologist*, Vol. 27, No. 2, pp. 51-92.

Pond, Alonzo W.
884.   1937   "Wisconsin joins the ranks of oldest inhabited areas in America". *Wisconsin Archeologist*, Vol. 17, No. 3, pp. 51-54.

Pope, Gustavus D., Jr.
885.   1956   "A preliminary stone point chronology for eastern Connecticut". *Eastern States Archeological Federation, Bulletin* No. 15, pp. 15-16.

Potter, Martha A.
886.   1964   "Some Paleo-Indian artifacts from Miami County, Ohio". *Ohio Archaeologist*, Vol. 14, No. 1, pp. 8-10.

Potter, Stephen R.
887.   1968   "A report on some Paleo-Indian projectile points from Virginia and nearby states". *Archeological Society of Virginia, Quarterly Bulletin*, Vol. 23, No. 1, pp. 11-19.

Powell, Bernard W.
888.   1971   "First site synthesis and proposed chronology for the aborigines of southwestern Connecticut". *Pennsylvania Archaeologist*, Vol. 41, Nos. 1-2, pp. 30-37.

Powell, J.W.
889.   1893   "Are there evidences of man in the glacial gravels?" *Popular Science Monthly*, Vol. 43, pp. 316-326.

Powell, Louis H.
890.   1957   "Browns Valley and Milnesand similarities". *American Antiquity*, Vol. 22, pp. 298-300.

Prahl, Earl J.
891.   1966   "The Muskegon River survey: 1965 and 1966". *Michigan Archaeologist*, Vol. 12, No. 4, pp. 183-209.

Praus, Alexis A.
892.   1964   "Bibliography of Michigan archaeology". *Anthropological Papers*, No. 22, *Museum of Anthropology*, University of Michigan, 77 pp.

Pritchard, James G.

893. 1964 "Quail Spring Paleo occupation site, Princess Anne County, Virginia". *The Chesopiean*, Vol. 2, No. 3, pp. 60-61.

Prufer, Olaf H.

894. 1959 "Evidence for Early Man in Ohio". *Cleveland Museum of Natural History, Museum News*, Vol. I, pp. 48-51.

895. 1960a "Early Man east of the Mississippi". In, *Steinzeit fragen der Alten und Neuen Welt*, Bonn, pp. 421-455. Also, reprinted by the Cleveland Museum of Natural History.

896. 1960b "Survey of Ohio fluted points, numbers 1, 2, and 3". Cleveland Museum of Natural History, Cleveland.

897. 1960c "An early lithic point from Twinsburg, Ohio". *Ohio Archaeologist*, Vol. 10, pp. 99-100.

898. 1961 "The Paleo-Indian problem in Ohio". *Ohio Archaeologist*, Vol. 11, No. 3, pp. 90-92.

899. 1962a "Fluted points and Ohio prehistory". *The Explorer*, Vol. 4, No. 3, pp. 14-21.

900. 1962b "Comments on, "The Paleo-Indian tradition in eastern North America", by Ronald J. Mason. In, *Current Anthropology*, Vol. 3, No. 3, Chicago, pp. 261-262.

901. 1962c "A reworked Paleo-Indian point from Sandusky County, Ohio". *Ohio Archaeologist*, Vol. 12, No. 3/4, pp. 82-83.

902. 1963a "Ice Age overkill". *The Explorer*, Vol. 5, No. 6, pp. 7-13.

903. 1963b "Survey of Ohio fluted points, no. 9". Cleveland Museum of Natural History, Cleveland.

904. 1963c "The McConnell Site: A late Palaeo-Indian workshop in Coshocton County, Ohio". *Scientific Publications of the Cleveland Museum of Natural History*, N.S., Vol. 2, No. 1, 51 pp.

905. 1964 "The Ross County point, a comment". *Tennessee Archaeologist*, Vol. 20, No. 2, pp. 80-81.

906. 1966a "The Mud Valley site: A late Palaeo-Indian locality in Holmes County, Ohio". *Ohio Journal of Science*, Vol. 66, No. 1, [68]-75 pp.

907. 1966b "Some reflections on the extinction of the Pleistocene megafauna". In, *Studies in Prehistory*, Sen and Ghosh (Editors), Firma K.L. Mukhopadhyay, Calcutta, pp. 28-40.

908. 1967 "The Scioto Valley archaeological survey". In, *Studies in Ohio Archaeology*, Olaf H. Prufer, and Douglas H. McKenzie (Editors). The Press of Western Reserve University, Cleveland, pp. 267-328.

Prufer, Olaf H., and Raymond S. Baby
909. 1963 "Palaeo-Indians of Ohio". Ohio Historical Society, Columbus, 68 pp.

Prufer, Olaf H., and G.W. Chinn
910. 1960 "Survey of Ohio fluted points, no. 2". Cleveland Museum of Natural History, Cleveland.

Prufer, Olaf H., and E.C. Munro
911. 1961 "Survey of Ohio fluted points, no. 5 and no. 6". Cleveland Museum of Natural History, Cleveland.

Prufer, Olaf H., and Charles Sofsky
912. 1965 "The McKibben Site (33TR-57), Trumball County, Ohio: A contribution to the late Paleo-Indian and Archaic phases of Ohio". *Michigan Archaeologist*, Vol. 11, No. 1, pp. 9-40.

Putnam, F.W.
913. 1884 "Human under-jaw found in gravel at Trenton, N.J.". *Proceedings of the American Antiquarian Society*, N.S., Vol. 3, 1884, p. 2. Also, *Winsor Collection*, Papers Nos. 4, 5, 6, Vol. 3.

914. 1888 "Paleolithic man in east and central North America. Part *III*". Peabody Museum of American Archaeology and Ethnology, Cambridge.

915. 1890 "Concluding remarks by the President, with illustrations of Paleolithic implements from Delaware, Indiana, New Jersey, and Minnesota. *Proceedings of the Boston Society of Natural History*, Vol. 24, pp. 158-165. Same in, *Paleolithic man in eastern and central North America, Part III*, Cambridge, Massachusetts, 1889.

916. 1898 "Early Man of the Delaware Valley". *Proceedings of the American Association for the Advancement of Science*, 1897, Vol. 46, pp. 344-348.

917. 1899 "Exploration of the Trenton gravels and of the Delaware Valley". *Annual Report of the American Museum of Natural History*, pp. 15-16.

Quimby, George Irving
918. 1952 "The archeology of the Upper Great Lakes area". In, *Archeology of eastern United States*, James B. Griffin (Editor), University of Chicago Press, Chicago, pp. 99-107.

919. 1956 "The Locus of the Natchez pelvis find". *American Antiquity*, Vol. 22, No. 1, pp. 77-79.

920. 1958 "Fluted points and geochronology of the Lake Michigan basin". *American Antiquity*, Vol. 23, No. 3, pp. 247-254.

921. 1959 "Lanceolate points and fossil beaches in the Upper Great Lakes region". *American Antiquity*, Vol. 24, No. 4, pp. 424-426.

922. 1962 Comments on "The Paleo-Indian tradition in eastern North America", by Ronald J. Mason. In, *Current Anthropology*, Vol. 3, No. 3, Chicago, p. 262.

923. 1963 "A new look at geochronology in the Upper Great Lakes region". *American Antiquity*, Vol. 28, No. 4, pp. 558-559.

924. 1965 *Indian life in the Upper Great Lakes, 11,000 B.C. to A.D. 1800.* University of Chicago Press, Chicago, 182 pp.

Raemsch, Bruce E.
925. 1968 "Artifacts from mid-Wisconsin gravels near Oneonta, New York". *Yager Museum Publications in Anthropology*, Bulletin 1, 8 pp.

926. 1970 "Projectile points from late Pleistocene gravels". *Anthropological Journal of Canada*, Vol. 8, No. 2, pp. 16-20.

Rau, Charles
927. 1873 "North American stone implements". *Annual Report of the Smithsonian Institution for 1872*, pp. 395-408..

Redfield, Alden
928. 1971 "Dalton project notes Vol. 1". University of Missouri, Museum of Anthropology, Columbia.

Retzek, Henry
929. 1935 "Human remains in gravel near West Union, Minnesota". *Science*, N.S., Vol. 82, p. 60.

Reynolds, Carl C.
930. 1955 "Huron County collection". *Ohio Archaeologist* 5, pp. 42-43.

Richards, Darrel J.
931. 1959 "Fluted points in Michigan". *Totem Pole*, Vol. XLII, No. 3, Aboriginal Research Club, Detroit, Michigan, March, 11 unnumbered pp., 11 illustrations.

932. 1962 "Paleo points". *Totem Pole*, Vol. XLV, No. 3, pp. 2-7.

Richards, Horace G.

933.   1939   "Reconsideration of the dating of the Abbott Farm Site at Trenton, New Jersey". *American Journal of Science*, Vol. 237, No. 5, pp. 345-354.

Ridley, Frank

934.   1954   "The Frank Bay Site, Lake Nipissing, Ontario". *American Antiquity*, Vol. 20, No. 1, pp. 40-50..

Ritchie, William A.

935.   1940   "Two prehistoric village sites at Brewerton, New York: Type components of the Brewerton focus, Laurentian aspect". *Researches and Transactions of the New York State Archaeological Association*, Vol. IX, No. 1, Rochester.

936.   1944   "The pre-Iroquoian occupations of New York State". *Rochester Museum of Arts and Sciences*, Memoir No. 1, 416 pp.

937.   1951   "Current concepts of continuity and chronology in New York prehistory". *Eastern States Archeological Federation, Bulletin*, No. 10, p. 5.

938.   1953   "A probable Paleo-Indian site in Vermont". *American Antiquity*, Vol. 18, No. 3, pp. 249-258.

939.   1956   "Prehistoric settlement patterns in northeastern North America". In, *Prehistoric settlement patterns in the New World*, Gordon R. Willey (Editor), Viking Fund Publications in Anthropology, No. 23, pp. 72-80.

940.   1957   "Traces of Early Man in the northeast". *New York State Museum and Science Service, Bulletin* 358, University of the State of New York, 91 pp.

941.   1958a   "An introduction to Hudson Valley prehistory". *New York State Museum and Science Service, Bulletin* No. 367, 112 pp.

942.   1958b   "The Paleo-Indian in the northeast". *Massachusetts Archeological Society, Bulletin*, Vol. 19, No. 2, pp. 21-22.

943.   1961   "A typology and nomenclature for New York projectile points". *New York State Museum and Science Service, Bulletin* No. 384, Albany.

944.   1965   *The archeology of New York State.* American Museum of Natural History, Natural History Press, Garden City, New York.

945.   1969a   *The archaeology of Martha's Vineyard. A framework for the prehistory of southern New England.* Natural History Press, Garden City, New York, 253 pp.

946. 1969b *The archaeology of New York State.* Revised edition, American Museum of Natural History, Natural History Press, Garden City, New York.

947. 1971 "A typology and nomenclature for New York projectile points". *New York State Museum and Science Service, Bulletin* No. 384 (revised 1961 edition), 132 pp.

Ritchie, William A. and Robert E. Funk
948. 1969 Comments on, "Archaeology studies in central New York". In, *New York Glaciogram,* Vol. 4, No. 1, pp. 13-16.

949. 1973 "Aboriginal settlement patterns in the northeast". *New York State Museum and Science Service,* Memoir 20, Albany, New York.

Ritzenthaler, Robert E.
950. 1966 "The Kouba Site: Paleo-Indians in Wisconsin". *Wisconsin Archeologist,* N.S. Vol. 47, No. 4, pp. 171-187.

951. 1967 "A cache of Paleo-Indian gravers from the Kouba Site". *Wisconsin Archeologist,* N.S., Vol. 48, No. 3, pp. 261-262.

952. 1970 "Clovis and Sandia-like points from Dane County, Wisconsin". *Wisconsin Archeologist,* N.S., Vol. 51, No. 1, pp. 261-262.

Ritzenthaler, Robert E. and Paul Scholz
953. 1951 "Folsomoid points in Wisconsin." *Wisconsin Archeologist,* N.S., Vol. 32, No. 2, pp. 45-48.

Robbins, Maurice
954. 1964a "A preliminary report of the Wapanucket #8 Site, Middleboro, Massachusetts". *Eastern States Archeological Federation, Bulletin,* No. 23, p. 13.

955. 1964b "A preliminary report of the Wapanucket #8 Site". *New World Antiquity,* Vol. 11, No. 7/8, pp. 79-94.

Robbins, Maurice and George A. Agogino
956. 1964 "The Wapanucket No. 8 Site: A Clovis-Archaic site in Massachusetts". *American Antiquity,* "Facts and Comments", Vol. 29, No. 4, pp. 509-513.

Roberts, Frank Harold Hanna, Jr.
957. 1936 "The significance of Folsom points east of the Mississippi". *Archaeological Society of Delaware, Bulletin,* Vol. 2, No. 4, p. 3a.

958. 1938 "The Folsom problem in American archeology". *Smithsonian Institution Annual Report for 1938,* pp. 531-546.

959. 1940 "Developments in the problem of the North American Paleo-Indian". *Smithsonian Miscellaneous Collections*, Vol. 100, pp. 51-116.

960. 1941 "Early Man search in Virginia". *El Palacio*, Vol. 48. p. 148.

961. 1945 "The New World Paleo-Indian". *Smithsonian Institute, Annual Report for 1944*, pp. 403-433.

962. 1951 "Radiocarbon dates and Early Man". In, "Radiocarbon dating", assembled by Frederick Johnson. *Memoirs* of the Society for American Archaeology, No. 8, pp. 20-22. Supplement to *American Antiquity*, Vol. 17, No. 1, Part 2.

963. 1953a "Earliest men in America. Their survival and spread in late Pleistocene and post-Pleistocene times". *Journal of World History*, Vol. 1, pp. 225-227.

964. 1953b "Recent developments in the Early Man problem in the New World". *Eastern States Archeological Federation, Bulletin*, Vol. 12, pp. 9-11.

965. 1962 Comments on, "The Paleo-Indian tradition in eastern North America", by Ronald J. Mason. In, *Current Anthropology*, Vol. 3, No. 3, Chicago, pp. 262-263.

Roberts, V.G., Jr., and E.M. Harris

966. 1969 "Some cubic lithic tools presumed to be shell mound Archaic". *Journal of Alabama Archaeology*, Vol. 15, No. 1, pp. 20-34.

Robertson, Arthur

967. 1947 "The Folsom culture in Southside Virginia". *Archeological Society of Virginia, Quarterly Bulletin*, Vol. 2, No. 2, pp. 5-6.

968. 1954 "Comments on making casts of Virginia fluted points". *Archeological Society of Virginia, Quarterly Bulletin*, Vol. 8, No. 3, pp. 12-13.

Rogers, Edward S., and Murray H. Rogers

969. 1950 "Archaeological investigations of the region about Lake Mistassini and Albanel, Province of Quebec, 1948". *American Antiquity*, Vol. 15, No. 4, pp. 322-377.

Rolingson, Martha Ann

970. 1964 "Paleo-Indian culture in Kentucky". *Kentucky Studies in Anthropology* No. 2.

Rolingson, Martha Ann, and Douglas W. Schwartz

971. 1964 "Paleo-Indian problems in Kentucky". Proceedings of the Nineteenth Archaeological Conference, Moundsville, Alabama, *Southeastern Archaeological Conference, Bulletin* No. 1, pp. 42-48.

972. 1966 "Late Paleo-Indian and early Archaic manifestations in western Kentucky". *University of Kentucky Studies in Anthropology*, No. 3, University of Kentucky Press, Lexington.

Romer, Alfred S.
973. 1933 "Pleistocene vertebrates and their bearing on the problem of human antiquity in North America". In, *The American Aborigines, their origin and antiquity*, Diamond Jenness (Editor), Fifth Pacific Science Congress, Canada, University of Toronto Press, Toronto, pp. 47-83.

Roosa, William B.
974. 1961 "Michigan fluted point sites". *Michigan Archaeologist*, Vol. 7, No. 2, June, pp. 11-12.

975. 1962 Comments on, "The Paleo-Indian tradition in eastern North America", by Ronald J. Mason. In, *Current Anthropology*, Vol. 3, No. 3, Chicago, pp. 263-265.

976. 1963 "Some Michigan fluted point sites and types". *Michigan Archaeologist*, Vol. 9, No. 3, pp. 44-48.

977. 1965 "Some Great Lakes fluted point types". *Michigan Archaeologist*, Vol. 11, Nos. 3-4, pp. 89-102.

Roosa, William B. and S.L. Peckhan
978. 1954 "Notes on the third interglacial artifacts". *American Antiquity*, Vol. 19, No. 3, pp. 280-281.

Rouse, Irving
979. 1946 Report on "A reexamination of the fossil human skeletal remains from Melbourne, Florida, with further data on the Vero skull", by T. Dale Stewart. In, *American Journal of Science*, Vol. 244, No. 12, p. 864.

980. 1950a "Vero and Melbourne man: A cultural and chronological interpretation". *New York Academy of Science, Transactions*, 2nd. Series, Vol. 12, No. 7, pp. 220-224.

981. 1950b Report on, *Ancient man in North America*, by H.M. Wormington, 1949. In, *American Journal of Science*, Vol. 248, No. 7, pp. 518-519.

982. 1951a Report on *Early Man in the New World*, by Kenneth MacGowan, 1950. *American Journal of Science*, Vol. 249, No. 7, p. 547

983. 1951b *A survey of Indian River archeology, Florida*. Yale University Publications in Anthropology, No. 44, Yale University Press, New Haven, Connecticut, 263 pp.

984. 1953 "Culture sequence in Connecticut". *New Hampshire Archeologist*, No. 5, pp. 1-9.

Rovner, Irwin, and G.A. Agogino
985. 1969 "Minnesota man: Archaeology's fickle female". *Anthropological Journal of Canada*, Vol. 7, No. 1, pp. 2-12.

Royer, Russell
986. 1963 "A fluted point from Luzerne County, Pennsylvania". *Pennsylvania Archaeologist*, Vol. 33, No. 3, pp. 140-141.

Russell, Eber L.
987. 1952 "A fluted point from Chautauqua County, New York". *Archeological Newsletter*, No. 5, Pittsburgh, pp. 5-6.

Russell, Frank
988. 1899 "Human remains from the Trenton gravels". *American Naturalist*, Vol. 33, No. 386, pp. 143-153.

Russell, George E.
989. 1967 "Projectile point sequences in the southeast". *Anthropological Journal of Canada*, Vol. 5, No. 4, pp. 23-29.

Russell, George E., and W. Mike Howell
990. 1972 "What preceded Clovis?" *Central States Archaeological Journal*, Vol. 19, No. 1, pp. 9-13.

Salisbury, Rollin D.
991. 1898 "On the origin and age of the relic-bearing sand at Trenton, N.J.". *Proceedings of the American Association for the Advancement of Science*, 1897, Vol. 46, pp. 350-355.

Salwen, Bert
992. 1968 "Review of "Debert: A Palaeo-Indian site in Central Nova Scotia", by George F. MacDonald. In, *American Anthropologist*, Vol. 70, No. 6, pp. 1231-1233.

Salzer, Robert J., and Mark Stock
993. 1961 "A fluted point from Jefferson County". *Wisconsin Archeologist*, Vol. 42, N.S., No. 3, pp. 133-135.

Sanford, John T.
994. 1957 "Geological observations at the Sheguiandah Site". *The Canadian Field-Naturalist*, Vol. 71, No. 3, pp. 138-148.

995. 1971 "Sheguiandah reviewed". *Anthropological Journal of Canada*, Vol. 9, No. 1, pp. 2-15.

Sardeson, F.W.
996. 1938   "Saint Anthony Falls and Minnesota man". *Pan-American Geologist*, Vol. 69, pp. 92-100.

Sargent, Howard R., and Francois G. Ledoux
997. 1973   "Two fluted points from New England". *Man in the Northeast*, No. 5, pp. 67-68.

Sauer, Carl O.
998. 1957   "The end of the Ice Age and its witnesses". *Geographical Review*, Vol. 47, pp. 29-43.

Savage, Howard G.
999. 1971   "Faunal analysis of the Inverhuron Site (BbHj-16)". *Department of Anthropology, University of Toronto, Research Report*, No. 2, pp. 7-85.

Saxon, Walter
1000. 1973   "The Paleo-Indian on Long Island". *New York State Archeological Association, The Bulletin*, No. 57, pp. 1-11.

Sayles, E.B.
1001. 1962   Comments on "The Paleo-Indian tradition in eastern North America", by Ronald J. Mason. In, *Current Anthropology*, Vol. 3, No. 3, Chicago, pp. 265-267.

Schwartz, Douglas W.
1002. 1965   "The Paleo-Indian era: Distribution of finds". Proceedings of the Twentieth Southeastern Archaeological Conference, *Southeastern Archaeological Conference, Bulletin* No. 2, pp. 6-9.

Sears, William H.
1003. 1964   "The southeastern United States". In, *Prehistoric man in the New World*, Jesse Jennings and Edward Norbeck (Editors), pp. 259-287.

Sellards, E.H.
1004. 1916a   "On the discovery of fossil human remains in Florida in association with extinct vertebrates". *American Journal of Science*, 4th Series, Vol. 42, (Whole Number *CXCII*), No. 247, pp. 1-18.

1005. 1916b   "Human remains and associated fossils from the Pleistocene of Florida". *Florida Geological Survey, Eighth Annual Report*, pp. 121-160.

1006. 1916c   "Human remains from the Pleistocene of Florida". *Science*, N.S., Vol. 44, No. 1139, pp. 615-617.

1007. 1917a   "Further notes on human remains from Vero, Florida". *American Anthropologist*, N.S., Vol. 19, No. 2, pp. 239-251.

1008. 1917b "On the association of human remains and extinct vertebrates at Vero, Florida". *Journal of Geology*, Vol. 25, No. 1, pp. 4-24.

1009. 1917c "Note on the deposits containing human remains and artifacts at Vero, Florida". *Journal of Geology*, Vol. 25, No. 7, pp. 659-660.

1010. 1917d "Review of the evidence on which the human remains found at Vero, Florida, are referred to the Pleistocene". *Florida Geological Survey, Ninth Annual Report*, pp. 69-84.

1011. 1918 "The skull of a Pleistocene tapir including description of a new species and a note on the associated fauna and flora". *Florida State Geological Survey, 10th Annual Report*, pp. 57-70.

1012. 1919 "Literature relating to human remains and artifacts at Vero, Florida". *American Journal of Science*, 4th Series, Vol. 47, (Whole Number *CXCVII*), No. 281, pp. 358-360.

1013. 1937 "The Vero finds in the light of present knowledge". In, *Early Man:* As depicted by leading authorities at the International Symposium, The Academy of Natural Sciences, Philadelphia, March, 1937, George Grant MacCurdy (Editor). With Introduction by John C. Merriam. J.B. Lippincott Company, London, pp. 193-210.

1014. 1940 "Early Man in America: Index to localities, and selected bibliography". *Geological Society of America, Bulletin*, Vol. 51, No. 3, pp. 373-431.

1015. 1947 "Early Man in America, index to localities and selected bibliography, 1940-1945". *Geological Society of America, Bulletin*, Vol. 58, No. 10, pp. 955-977.

1016. 1952 *Early Man in North America: A study in prehistory.* Greenwood Press, Publishers, New York. University of Texas Press, Austin.

Shaler, N.S.
1017. 1877 "On the age of the Delaware gravel beds containing chipped pebbles". *Tenth Annual Report of the Trustees of the Peabody Museum,* American Archaeology and Ethnology, Vol. 2, No. 1, pp. 44-47.

1018. 1889 "The geology of Nantucket". *United States Geological Survey, Bulletin* 53, pp. 24-25.

1019. 1893 "Antiquity of man in eastern North America". *American Geologist*, Vol. 11, pp. 180-184.

Shane, Orrin C., III, and James L. Murphy
1020. 1967 "A survey of the Hocking Valley, Ohio". In, *Studies in Ohio*

Archaeology, Olaf H. Prufer and Douglas H. McKenzie (Editors), The Press of Western Reserve University, Cleveland, pp. 329-356.

Shay, C. Thomas

1021. 1971 "The Itasca bison kill site: An ecological analysis". *Minnesota Prehistoric Archaeology Series,* Publications of the Minnesota Historical Society.

Shetrone, H.C.

1022. 1936 "The Folsom phenomenon as seen from Ohio". *Ohio State Archeological and Historical Quarterly,* Vol. 45, No. 3, pp. 240-256.

Short, John T.

1023. 1880 *The North Americans of antiquity, their origin, migrations, and type of civilization considered.* Harper and Brothers, Publishers, New York.

Simpson, George Gaylord

1024. 1929a "Hunting extinct animals in Florida". *Natural History,* Vol. 29, pp. 506-518.

1025. 1929b "The extinct land mammals of Florida". *Florida Geological Survey,* 20th Annual Report, p. 268.

1026. 1930a "Additions to the Pleistocene of Florida". *American Museum Novitates,* American Museum of Natural History, No. 406, 14 pp.

1027. 1930b "Pleistocene mammalian fauna of the Seminole Field, Pinellas County, Florida". *American Museum of Natural History, Bulletin,* Vol. 56, pp. 569-572.

1028. 1931 "Origin of mammalian faunas as illustrated by that of Florida". *American Naturalist,* Vol. 65, pp. 258-276.

Simpson, J. Clarence

1029. 1948 "Folsom-like points from Florida". *Florida Anthropologist,* Vol. 1, pp. 11-15.

Simpson, Ruth D.

1030. 1946 "The seal was broken". *Masterkey,* Vol. 20, No. 5, pp. 154-156.

Skeels, Margaret Anne

1031. 1962 "The mastodons and mammoths of Michigan". *Papers of the Michigan Academy of Science, Arts, and Letters,* Vol. 47, pp. 101-133.

Smail, William

1032. 1951 "Some early projectile points from the St. Louis area". *Illinois State Archaeological Society,* N.S., Vol. 2, pp. 11-16.

Smith, Arthur George

1033. 1951a "Fluted points from Milan, Ohio". *Ohio Archaeologist*, Vol. 1, No. 3, pp. 30-31.

1034. 1951b "Fluted points from Milan, Ohio". *Southwestern Lore*, Vol. 17, No. 1.

1035. 1952 "A survey of fluted points in Ohio". *Ohio Archaeologist*, Vol. 2, No. 1, pp. 7-9.

1036. 1953 "Waterworn artifacts from late Pleistocene lake beaches in northern Ohio". *American Antiquity*, Vol. 19, No. 2, pp. 156-157.

1037. 1954a "Waterworn artifacts from late Pleistocene lake beaches in northern Ohio". *Ohio Archaeologist*, Vol. 4, No. 1, pp. 30-32.

1038. 1954b "A decadent Paleo-Indian complex on the Alabama River". *Tennessee Archaeologist*, Vol. 10, No. 2, pp. 66-67.

1039. 1955 "A possible Paleo-Indian site in north central Tennessee". *Tennessee Archaeologist*, Vol. 11, No. 1, pp. 21-23.

1040. 1956a "A very early Archaic or late Paleo-Indian type". *Ohio Archaeologist*, Vol. 6, p. 137.

1041. 1956b "Paleo-Indian tools from Ringgold Creek, Montgomery County, Tennessee". *Tennessee Archaeologist*, Vol. 12, No. 2, pp. 11-15.

1042. 1960 "The Sawmill Site, Erie County, Ohio". *Ohio Archaeologist*, Vol. 10, No. 3, pp. 84-97.

1043. 1961 "Trade or travel". *Ohio Archaeologist*, Vol. 11, No. 4, pp. 130-131.

1044. 1962 "Paleo-Indian knives". *Ohio Archaeologist*, Vol. 12, p. 108.

1045. 1965 "Nellie chert: A trait associated with Paleo-Indians". *Ohio Archaeologist*, Vol. 15, No. 1, pp. 6-7.

1046. 1967 "The very first Ohioans". *Ohio Archaeologist*, Vol. 17, No. 2, pp. 82-83.

Smith, Carlyle S.

1047. 1947 "An outline of the archeology of coastal New York". *Archeological Society of Connecticut, Bulletin*, No. 21, New Haven, pp. 2-9.

1048. 1950 "The archaeology of coastal New York". *American Museum of Natural History, Anthropological Papers*, Vol. 43, Part 2.

Smith, Harlan I.

1049. 1910 "An unknown field in American archaeology". *American Geographical Society, Bulletin,* Vol. 42, No. 7, pp. 511-521.

Smith, Ira F., III

1050. 1972 "Pennsylvania archaeology: An overview". *Eastern States Archeological Federation, Bulletin* No. 31, p. 14.

Smith, Philip E.L.

1051. 1961 "Fluted points in Paris". *American Antiquity,* Vol. 26, No. 3, Part I, pp. 428-431.

Soday, Frank J.

1052. 1952 "A new Paleo-Indian site". *The Record,* Dallas Archaeological Society, Vol. 11, pp 6-9.

1053. 1954 "The Quad Site: A Paleo-Indian village in Northern Alabama". *Tennessee Archaeologist,* Vol. 10, No. 1, pp. 1-19.

Solecki, Ralph S.

1054. 1954 "A fluted point from Dickson County, Tennessee". *Tennessee Archaeologist,* Vol. 10, pp. 63-65.

1055. 1961 "Early Man and changing sea levels, Popular Island, Maryland". *American Antiquity,* Vol. 27, No. 2, pp. 234-236.

Spier, Leslie

1056. 1916 "New data on the Trenton argillite culture". *American Anthropologist,* N.S., Vol. 18, No. 2, pp. 181-189.

1057. 1918 "The Trenton argillite culture". *American Museum of Natural History, Anthropological Papers,* Vol. 22, pp. 167-226.

Steeves, H.R., Jr.

1058. 1956 "A small collection of Paleo-American points from Alabama". *Tennessee Archaeologist,* Vol. 12, No. 2, pp. 22-27.

Steinbring, Jack, and J.P. Whelan

1059. 1971 "Test excavations at the Fish Lake Dam Site, Minnesota". *Minnesota Archaeologist,* Vol. XXXI, No. 1, pp. 3-40.

Sterns, F.H.

1060. 1918 "The Pleistocene man of Vero, Florida, a summary of the evidence of man's antiquity in the New World". *Scientific American Supplement,* Vol. 85, No. 2214, pp. 354-355.

1061. 1919 "The Pleistocene man of Vero, Florida, a review of the latest evidence and theories". *Scientific American Supplement,* Vol. 87, No. 2251, pp. 118-119.

Stewart, T.D.

1062. 1946 "A reexamination of the fossil human skeletal remains from Melbourne, Florida, with further data on the Vero skull". *Smithsonian Miscellaneous Collection*, Vol. 106, No. 10, 28 pp.

1063. 1951 "Antiquity of man in America demonstrated by the flourine test". *Science*, Vol. 113, No. 2936, pp. 391-392.

Stoltman, James B.

1064. 1966 Review of "The Paleo-Indian occupation of the Holcombe Beach", by James E. Fitting, Jerry DeVisscher, and Edward J. Wahla. *Anthropological Papers, Museum of Anthropology*, No. 27, University of Michigan, 1966. In, *Wisconsin Archeologist*, New Series, Vol. 47, No. 4, pp. 214-218.

1065. 1971 "Prismatic blades from northern Minnesota". *Plains Anthropologist*, Vol. 16, No. 52, pp. 105-110.

Stoltman, James B., and Karen Workman

1066. 1969 "A preliminary study of Wisconsin fluted points". *Wisconsin Archeologist*, N.S., Vol. 50, No. 4, pp. 189-214.

Storck, Peter L.

1067. 1970 "Beachcombing into the past". *Royal Ontario Museum, Archaeological Newsletter*, New Series, No. 63, August, Toronto, 4 pp.

1068. 1971 "The search for Early Man in Ontario". *Rotunda*, The Bulletin of the Royal Ontario Museum, Vol. 4, No. 4, pp. 18-27.

1069. 1972a "An householder, which bringeth forth out of his treasure things new and old. St. Matthew 13.52". *Royal Ontario Museum, Archaeological Newsletter*, New Series, No. 80, January, Toronto, 4 pp.

1070. 1972b "An unusual late Paleo-Indian projectile point from Grey County, southern Ontario". *Ontario Archaeology*, No. 18, pp. 37-45.

1071. 1973 "Two Paleo-Indian projectile points from the Bronte Creek gap, Halton County, Ontario". *Archaeology Paper* No. 1, *Royal Ontario Museum*, 4 pp.

Stuckenrath, Robert, Jr.

1072. 1964 "The Debert Site: Early Man in the northeast". *Expedition*, Vol. 7, No. 1, Bulletin of the University Museum, University of Pennsylvania, pp. 20-29.

1073. 1966 "The Debert archaeological project, Nova Scotia: Radiocarbon dating". *Tirage a part de Quaternia, VIII*, Roma.

Sugden, Earl

1074. 1954 "Folsomoid points in Richland County". *Wisconsin Archeologist,* N.S., Vol. 35, No. 4, pp. 79-81.

Taylor, Fayne G.

1075. 1957 "Early chipped flint objects from west Tennessee". *Tennessee Archaeologist,* Vol. 13, No. 2, pp. 81-87.

Taylor, William E., Jr.

1076. 1964a "La préhistoire de la péninsula du Labrador". *Anthropology Papers,* No. 7, *National Museum of Canada,* 33 pp.

1077. 1964b "The prehistory of the Quebec-Labrador peninsula". In, *Le Nouveau Quebec,* by Jean Malaurie and Jacques Rousseau, Paris and La Haye, pp. 181-206.

Thiel, George A.

1078. 1936a "Pleistocene geology of the sediments in which the Minnesota man was discovered". Abstract, *Proceedings of the Minnesota Academy of Science,* Vol. 4, pp. 65-68.

1079. 1936b "The Pleistocene geology of the Prairie Lake region". In, *Pleistocene man in Minnesota,* by Albert E. Jenks. University of Minnesota Press, Minneapolis, pp. 17-33.

Thomas, Edward S.

1080. 1952 "The Orleton Farms mastodon". *Ohio Journal of Science,* Vol. 52, No. 1, pp. 1-5.

Thomas, Ronald A.

1081. 1966 "Paleo-Indian in Delaware". *Delaware Archaeology,* Vol. 2, No. 3, pp. 1-11.

Thompson, Ben W.

1082. 1971 "The 1970 Koster Site". *Central States Archaeological Journal,* Vol. 18, No. 3, pp. 100-107.

Thruston, Gates P.

1083. 1890 *The antiquities of Tennessee.* Robert Clarke and Company, Cincinnati.

Timlin, Joseph P., and B.E. Raemsch

1084. 1971 "Pleistocene tools from the northeast of North America; the Timlin Site". *Yager Museum Publications in Anthropology, Bulletin,* No. 3, 21 pp.

Traver, Jerome D.

1085. 1963 "Paleo artifacts from northeastern North Carolina". *Archeological Society of Virginia, Quarterly Bulletin,* Vol. 18, No. 2, pp. 35-36.

Trickey, E. Bruce, and Nicholas H. Holmes, Jr.
1086. 1971 "A chronological framework for the Mobile Bay region". *Journal of Alabama Archaeology*, Vol. 17, No. 2, pp. 115-128.

Troup, Charles E., and Daniel Josselyn
1087. 1967 "Pebble tools from the Weiss Reservoir". *Journal of Alabama Archaeology*, Vol. 13, No. 1, pp. 56-60.

Upham, Warren
1088. 1884 "Glacial geology of Little Falls, Minnesota area". In, "Vestiges of Early Man in Minnesota", *American Naturalist*, Vol. 18, pp. 706-708.

1089. 1888 "The recession of the ice-sheet in Minnesota and its relation to the gravel deposits overlying the quartz implements found by Miss Babbitt at Little Falls, Minnesota". *Proceedings of the Boston Society for Natural History*, Vol. 23, pp. 436-447.

1090. 1893 "Man and the glacial period". *American Geologist*, Vol. 11, pp. 189-191.

1091. 1902 "Man in the Ice Age at Lansing, Kansas, and Little Falls, Minnesota". *American Geologist*, Vol. 30, pp. 135-150.

Vallois, H.V.
1092. 1934 "Un nouvel 'homme fossile' en Amérique: l'homme du Minnesota". *L'Anthropologie*, t. 44, pp. 218-220.

Van Hoesen, Paul
1093. 1960 "The (De-U-No-Dil-Lo) fluted culture from ten thousand years along the Unadilla". *The Bulletin, New York State Archeological Association*, No. 20, pp. 14-18.

Van Male, W.C.
1094. 1936 "An interesting anthropological find from the Lake Michigan region". *Transactions of the Illinois State Academy of Science*, Vol. 29, pp. 52-53.

Vaughan, Thomas Wayland
1095. 1917 "On reported Pleistocene human remains at Vero, Florida". *Journal of Geology*, Vol. 25, No. 1, pp. 40-42.

Volk, Ernest
1096. 1911 "The archaeology of the Delaware Valley". *Papers of the Peabody Museum of American Archaeology and Ethnology*, Vol. 5, Harvard University, 258 pp., 125 plates.

Wachtel, H.C.
1097. 1954 "The mammoth in Ohio". *The Ohio Archaeologist*, Vol. 4, No. 2, pp. 6-9.

Waddell, Eugene C.

1098. 1965 "South Carolina fluted points". In, *Proceedings of the Southeastern Archaeological Conference, 20th, 1963, Macon, Georgia.* Southeastern Archaeological Conference, Bulletin *No. 2, Cambridge, Massachusetts, pp. 52-54.*

Wadsworth, M.

1099. 1881 "On the lithological character of the implements from the gravel at Trenton, N.J." *Winsor Collection,* Vol. 3, Paper No. 11.

Wagner, Louis

1100. 1967 "Rare spear find". *Central States Archaeological Journal,* Vol. 14, No. 1, p. 21.

Wahla, Edward J.

1101. 1959 (No title) report on two fluted points illustrated from Michigan. *Chips from the Totel Pole,* Aboriginal Research Club, Detroit, Michigan, November, 1 p., 1 illustration.

1102. 1961a (No title) report on Clovis type points and other artifacts from Paleo Site 2, Holcombe Beach. *Chips from the Totel Pole,* Aboriginal Research Club, Detroit, Michigan, May, 1 p., 1 illustration.

1103. 1961b "The Holcombe Paleo-Indian site". *The Totem Pole,* Vol. 44, No. 7, October, Aboriginal Research Club, Detroit, Michigan, 3, unnumbered pp., 1 illustration.

1104. 1961c "A Paleo-Indian site in S.E. Michigan". *The Coffinberry News Bulletin,* Vol. *VIII,* No. 6, Wright L. Coffinberry Chapter, Michigan Archaeological Society, Grand Rapids, Michigan, June, pp. 69-71, 1 illustration.

1105. 1962a (No title) report illustrating additional artifacts found at Paleo Site No. 2, Holcombe Beach, Sterling Township, Macomb County. *Chips from the Totem Pole,* Aboriginal Research Club, Detroit, Michigan, January, 1 p., 1 illustration.

1106. 1962b (No title) report on additional finds at or in the vicinity of Paleo Site No. 2, Holcombe Beach. *Chips from the Totem Pole,* Aboriginal Research Club, Detroit, Michigan, May, 1 p., 1 illustration.

1107. 1962c "Report on DeVisscher Paleo 2 Site". *The Totem Pole,* Supplementary Bulletin, Aboriginal Research Club, Detroit, Michigan, October, 2 unnumbered pp., 2 illustrations.

1108. 1962d (No title) report on additional work done at Paleo Site No. 2, Holcombe Beach. *Chips from the Totem Pole.* Aboriginal Research Club, Detroit, Michigan, November, 1 p., 1 illustration.

1109. 1963 (No title) brief mention of mammoth bones in Berrien County. *Chips from the Totem Pole*, Aboriginal Research Club, Detroit, Michigan, April, p. 1.

1110. 1967 "Holcombe caribou people in the light of studies of similar surviving hunters". *Totem Pole*, Vol. 50, No. 1, pp. 3-8.

Wahla, Edward J., and Jerry DeVisscher

1111. 1969 "The Holcombe Paleo-point". *Michigan Archaeologist*, Vol. 15, No. 4, pp. 109-111.

Wallace, Alfred Russell

1112. 1887 "The antiquity of man in North America". *Nineteenth Century*, Vol. 22, pp. 667-679.

Waller, Ben I.

1113. 1969 "Paleo-Indian and other artifacts from a Florida stream bed". *Florida Anthropologist*, Vol. 22, Nos. 1-4, pp. 37-39.

1114. 1970 "Some occurrences of Paleo-Indian projectile points in Florida waters". *Florida Anthropologist*, Vol. 23, No. 4, pp. 129-134.

1115. 1971 "Hafted flake knives". *Florida Anthropologist*, Vol. 24, No. 4, pp. 173-174.

1116. 1972 "Some occurrences of Paleo-Indian projectile points in Florida waters". Abstract, Paper given at the 1971 annual meeting of the *Eastern States Archeological Federation*, Bulletin 31, pp. 14-15.

Waring, A.J., Jr.

1117. 1961 "Fluted points on the South Carolina coast". *American Antiquity*, Vol. 26, No. 4, pp. 550-552.

Warren, Lyman O.

1118. 1966 "A possible Paleo-Indian site in Pinellas County". *Florida Anthropologist*, Vol. 19, No. 1, pp. 39-41.

1119. 1968 "Caladesi Causeway: A possible inundated Paleo-Indian workshop". *Florida Anthropologist*, Vol. 21, Nos. 2-3, pp. 92-94.

1120. 1970 "The Kellogg fill from Boca Ciega Bay, Pinellas County, Florida". *Florida Anthropologist*, Vol. 23, No. 4, pp. 163-167.

Warren, Lyman O., and Ripley P. Bullen

1121. 1965 "A Dalton Complex from Florida". *Florida Anthropologist*, Vol. 18, No. 1, pp. 29-32.

Waters, Joseph H.

1122. 1962 "How early post-Wisconsin man came to New England".

Massachusetts Archaeological Society, Bulletin, Vol. 23, No. 2, pp. 21-26.

Waters, Spencer A.

1123.   1957   "Paleo Indian artifacts from collections in North Alabama". *Tennessee Archaeologist*, Vol. 13, No. 1, pp. 49-54.

1124.   1959   "Red Hill, a Dalton site". *Journal of Alabama Archaeology*, Vol. 5, No. 3, pp. 77-82.

Wauchope, Robert

1125.   1939   "Fluted points from South Carolina". *American Antiquity*, "Facts and Comments", Vol. 4, No. 4, pp. 344-346.

1126.   1966   "Archaeological survey of northern Georgia. With a test of some cultural hypotheses". *Society for American Archaeology, Memoir* 21.

Webb, C.H.

1127.   1948   "Evidence of pre-pottery cultures in Louisiana". *American Antiquity*, Vol. 13, No. 3, pp. 227-232.

Webb, Raymond

1128.   1972   "A here-to-fore unclassified stone tool". *Florida Anthropologist*, Vol. 25, No. 1, pp. 47-48.

Webb, William S.

1129.   1950   "The Carlson Annis mound site 5 Butler County, Kentucky". *University of Kentucky, Reports in Anthropology*, Vol. 7, No. 4, Lexington.

1130.   1951   "The Parrish Village Site, site 45 Hopkins County, Kentucky". *University of Kentucky, Reports in Anthropology*, Vol. 7, No. 6, Lexington.

Webb, William S., and W.D. Funkhouser

1131.   1934   "The occurrence of the fossil remains of Pleistocene vertebrates in the caves of Barren County, Kentucky". *University of Kentucky, Reports in Archaeology and Anthropology*, Vol. 3, No. 2, 65 pp.

Wesley, William H.

1132.   1967   "Site report 40GL-1 Giles County, Tennessee". *Tennessee Archaeologist*, Vol. 23, No. 2, pp. 45-57.

1133.   1968   "The 'Broken Rock' Site". *Journal of Alabama Archaeology*, Vol. 14, No. 2, pp. 62-69.

1134.   1970   "The large chopper scraper". *Anthropological Journal of Canada*, Vol. 8, No. 3, pp. 11-13.

Wheat, Joe Ben
1135.   1971   "Lifeways of Early Man in North America". *Arctic Anthropology*, Vol. *VIII*, No. 2, pp. 22-31.

Whitmore, Frank C., Jr., K.O. Emery, H.B.S. Cooke, and Donald J.P. Swift
1136.   1967   "Elephant teeth from the Atlantic coastal shelf". *Science*, Vol. 156, No. 3781, pp. 1477-1481.

Wickham, H.F.
1137.   1919   "Fossil beetles from Vero, Florida". *Florida Geological Survey, Twelfth Annual Report*, pp. 5-8. Also in, *American Journal of Science*, 4th Series, Vol. *XLVII*, No. 281, pp. 355-357.

Wieland, G.R.
1138.   1918   "The Vero Man and the sabre tooth". *Science*, N.S., Vol. 48, No. 1230, pp. 93-94.

Wilford, Lloyd A.
1139.   1941   "A tentative classification of the prehistoric cultures of Minnesota". *American Antiquity*, Vol. 6, No. 3, pp. 231-249.

1140.   1942   "Minnesota archaeology: Current explorations and concepts". *Proceedings of the Minnesota Academy of Science*, Vol. 10, pp. 20-26.

1141.   1955   "A revised classification of the prehistoric cultures of Minnesota". *American Antiquity*, Vol. 21, No. 2, pp. 130-142.

Wilkins, E.S.
1142.   1969   "An unfinished fluted point from New Castle County, Delaware". *Archaeological Society of Delaware, Bulletin*, No. 7, pp. 27-30.

Wilkinson, Elizabeth M.
1143.   1966   "Paleo-Indian components of the Flint Run Jasper Quarry Site 44-WC-1, Shenandoah, Valley of Virginia". *The Chesopiean*, Vol. 4, No. 4, pp. 90-110.

Willey, Gordon R.
1144.   1961   "New World prehistory". *Annual Report of the Smithsonian Institution for 1960*, pp. 551-575. Also, *Science*, Vol. 131, No. 3393, 1960, pp. 73-86.

1145.   1966   *An introduction to American archaeology, Volume One, North and Middle America.* Prentice-Hall Incorporated, Englewood Cliffs, New Jersey.

Williams, Ernest H., Jr., and Daniel W. Josselyn
1146.   1970   "Flake point". *Journal of Alabama Archaeology*, "Facts and Comments", Vol. 16, No. 2, p. 134.

Williams, Stephen

1147. 1956 "Settlement patterns in the lower Mississippi Valley". In, *Prehistoric settlement patterns in the New World*, Gordon R. Willey (Editor), Viking Fund Publications in Anthropology, No. 23, pp. 52-62.

1148. 1957 "The Island 35 mastodon: its bearing on the age of Archaic cultures in the east". *American Antiquity*, Vol. 22, No. 4, pp. 359-372.

Williams, Stephen, and James B. Stoltman

1149. 1965 "An outline of southeastern United States prehistory with particular emphasis on the Paleo-Indian Era". In, *The Quaternary of the United States*, H.E. Wright and David G. Frey (Editors), Princeton University Press, pp. 669-683.

Wilmsen, Edwin N.

1150. 1965 "An outline of Early Man studies in the United States". *American Antiquity*, Vol. 31, No. 2, Part 1, pp. 172-192.

1151. 1968a "Paleo-Indian site utilization". In, *Anthropological archeology in the Americas*, Betty J. Meggers (Editor), The Anthropological Society of Washington, pp. 22-40.

1152. 1968b "Lithic analysis in Paleoanthropology". *Science*, Vol. 161, No. 3845, pp. 982-987.

1153. 1970 "Lithic analysis and cultural inference: A Paleo-Indian case". *Anthropological Papers*, No. 16, University of Arizona, 87 pp.

Wilson, Thomas

1154. 1890a "A study of prehistoric anthropology. A hand-book for beginners". *Annual Report of the Smithsonian Institution for 1889*, pp. 597-671.

1155. 1890b "Results of an inquiry as to the existence of man in North America during the Paleolithic period of the Stone Age". *Annual Report of the Smithsonian Institution for 1889*, pp. 677-702.

1156. 1892 "Man and mylodon: Their possible contemporaneous existence in the Mississippi Valley". *American Naturalist*, Vol. 26, No. 307, pp. 628-631.

1157. 1893 "Primitive industry". *Annual Report of the Smithsonian Institution for 1892*, pp. 521-534.

1158. 1894 "Primitive industry". *The Archaeologist*, Vol. II, No. 8, pp. 238-246.

1159. 1898 "Investigation in the sand-pits of Lalor Field, near Trenton, New Jersey". *American Association for the Advancement of Science*, Vol. 46, pp. 381-383.

1160. 1898   "Prehistoric art; or, the origin of art as manifested in the works of prehistoric man". *Annual Report of the Smithsonian Institution for 1897*, pp. 349-664.

Winchell, N.H.

1161. 1911   *The Aborigines of Minnesota.* Minnesota Historical Society, 761 pp.

1162. 1913   "The weathering of Aboriginal stone artifacts". *Minnesota Historical Society Collection,* Vol. 16, Part 1, 186 pp.

Winn, Vetal

1163. 1928   "Two fluted stone implements". *Wisconsin Archeologist,* N.S., Vol. 7, pp. 219-221.

Winters, Howard D.

1164. 1959   "The Paleo-Indian period". *Illinois Archaeological Survey, Bulletin* 1, pp. 5-8.

1165. 1962   "Distributional patterns of fluted points in southern Illinois". *Council for Illinois Archaeology, Report* No. 10, Illinois State Museum.

1166. 1967   "An archaeological survey of the Wabash Valley in Illinois". *Illinois State Museum Report of Investigations,* No. 10, 95 pp.

Wissler, Clark

1167. 1916   "The application of statistical methods to the data on the Trenton argillite culture". *American Anthropologist,* Vol. 18, No. 2, pp. 190-198.

Witthoft, John

1168. 1946   "Smoothed-base projectile points from eastern Pennsylvania". *Pennsylvania Archaeologist,* Vol. 16, No. 4, pp. 123-129.

1169. 1950a "The history and present status of Pennsylvania archeology". *Proceedings of the American Philosophical Society,* Vol. 94, No. 3, pp. 301-307.

1170. 1950b "Notes on Pennsylvania fluted points". *Pennsylvania Archaeologist,* Vol. 20, pp. 49-54.

1171. 1952   "A Paleo-Indian site in eastern Pennsylvania: An early hunting culture". *Proceedings of the American Philosophical Society,* Vol. 96, No. 4, Philadelphia, pp. 464-495.

1172. 1954   "A note on fluted point relationships". *American Antiquity,* "Facts and Comments", Vol. 19, No. 3, pp. 271-273.

1173. 1956 "Middle Woodland blade and core industries of the eastern United States". *Eastern States Archeological Federation, Bulletin*, No. 15, p. 11.

1174. 1961 "Notes on the Archaic cultures of the Appalachian Mountain region". *The Bulletin, New York State Archeological Association*, No. 21, pp. 7-15.

1175. 1962 Comments on, "The Paleo-Indian tradition in eastern North America", by Ronald J. Mason. In, *Current Anthropology*, Vol. 3, No. 3, Chicago, pp. 267-270.

Wittry, Warren L.

1176. 1964 "Earliest man in the Upper Great Lakes area". *Cranbrook Institute of Science News Letter*, Vol. 34, No. 3, Bloomfield Hills, Michigan, pp. 34-40.

1177. 1965 "The Institute digs a mastodon". *Cranbrook Institute of Science News Letter*, Vol. 35, No. 2, Bloomfield Hills, Michigan, pp. 14-19.

Wood, W. Raymond

1178. 1965 Review of, *Paleo-Indian culture in Kentucky*, by Martha A. Rolingson. In, *Missouri Archaeological Society Newsletter*, No. 191, p. 7.

Woolsey, John L.

1179. 1950 "Folsom-like point from Saltvilie, Ga." *Tennessee Archaeologist*, Vol. 6, No. 1, p. 12.

Wormington, Helen Marie

1180. 1957 *Ancient man in North America*. Denver Museum of Natural History Popular Series, No. 4, Denver, 322 pp.

1181. 1962 "A survey of early American prehistory". *American Scientist*, Vol. 50, No. 1, pp. 230-242.

1182. 1962 "Comments on, "Paleo-Indian tradition in eastern North America", by Ronald J. Mason. In, *Current Anthropology*, Vol. 3, No. 3, Chicago, pp. 270-271.

1183. 1966 "When did man come to North America". In, *Ancient hunters of the far west*, Richard F. Pourade (Editor), Union-Tribune Publishing Company, San Diego, pp. 109-124.

1184. 1967 "The Paleo-Indian". In, *The Philadelphia Anthropological Society; Papers presented on its golden anniversary*, Jacob W. Gruber (Editor), pp. 55-66.

1185. 1971 "Comments on Early Man in North America, 1960-1970". *Arctic Anthropology*, Vol. VIII, No. 2, pp. 83-91.

Wray, Donald E.
1186. 1952 "Archeology of the Illinois Valley: 1950". In, *Archeology of eastern United States*, James B. Griffin (Editor). The University of Chicago Press, Chicago, pp. 152-164.

Wright, A.A.
1187. 1893 "Older drift in the Delaware Valley". *American Geologist*, Vol. 11, pp. 184-186.

Wright, G. Frederick, D.D.
1188. 1882 "Glacial phenomena on the Delaware". *American Journal of Science*, Third Series, Vol. XXIII, (Whole Number CXXIII), No. 135, pp. 242-243.

1189. 1883 "An attempt to estimate the age of the Palaeolithic-bearing gravels in Trenton, New Jersey". *Proceedings of the Boston Society for Natural History*, Vol. 21, pp. 137-147.

1190. 1887 "The relation of the glacial period to archaeology in Ohio". *Ohio Archaeological and Historical Quarterly*, Vol. I, pp. 174-186.

1191. 1888a "On the age of the Ohio gravel beds". *Proceedings of the Boston Society for Natural History*, Vol. 23, pp. 427-436.

1192. 1888b "Preglacial man in Ohio". *Ohio Archaeological and Historical Society Publication*, Vol. 1, pp. 257-259.

1193. 1888c "On the age of the Ohio gravel beds". In, "Palaeolithic man in eastern and central North America", *Winsor Collection*, Vol. III, Paper No. 10, pp. 427-436.

1194. 1889 *The Ice Age in North America, and its bearings on the antiquity of man.* D. Appleton and Company, New York, 622 pp.,

1195. 1892 *Man and the glacial period*, with an appendix on tertiary man, by Henry W. Haynes, and Paul Kegan. Trench, Trübner and Company Limited, London, 385 pp, 111 illustrations and maps.

1196. 1893 "Evidences of glacial men in Ohio". *Popular Science Monthly*, Vol. 43, pp. 29-39.

1197. 1895 "New evidence of glacial man in Ohio". *Popular Science Monthly*, Vol. 48, No. 2, pp. 157-165.

1198. 1896 "Account of the discovery of a chipped chert implement in undisturbed glacial gravel near Steubenville, Ohio". *Proceedings of the American Association for the Advancement of Science*, Vol. 44, pp. 296-297.

1199. 1897 "Special explorations in the implement-bearing deposits on the Lalor Farm, Trenton, N.J." *Science*, N.S., Vol. 6, pp. 637-645.

1200. 1898 "Special explorations in the implement-bearing deposits on the Lalor Farm, Trenton, N.J." *Proceedings of the American Association for the Advancement of Science for 1897*, Vol. 46, pp. 355-364.

1201. 1899 "Correlation of the glacial deltas in the lower part of the Delaware and Susquehanna Rivers". *Proceedings of the American Association for the Advancement of Science for 1898*, Vol. 48, pp. 359-361.

1202. 1911 "Glacial man at Trenton, New Jersey". *Records of the Past*, Vol. 10, Part 5, pp. 273-282.

1203. 1912 *Origin and antiquity of man.* Bibliotheca Sacra Company, Oberlin, Ohio, pp. ix, 547, 42 illustrations.

Wright, H.E., Jr., and David G. Frey (Editors)
1204. 1965 *The Quaternary of the United States.* A review volume for the VIIth Congress of the International Association for Quaternary Research, Princeton University Press, Princeton, New Jersey.

Wright, Henry T., and William B. Roosa
1205. 1966 "The Barnes Site: A fluted point assemblage from the Great Lakes region". *American Antiquity*, Vol. 31, No. 6, pp. 850-860.

Wright, James V.
1206. 1963 "An archaeological survey along the north shore of Lake Superior". *Anthropology Papers*, No. 3, National Museum of Canada, 9 pp.

1207. 1968 "The Boreal forest". In, *Science, history, and Hudson Bay*, C.S. Beals (Editor). Department of Energy, Mines and Resources, Queen's Printer, Ottawa, pp. 55-68.

1208. 1969 "A program is needed to stop the destruction of prehistoric remains". *Science Forum*, Vol. 2, No. 5, pp. 12-14.

1209. 1972 *Ontario prehistory, an eleven-thousand-year archaeological outline.* Archaeological Survey of Canada, National Museum of Man, National Museums of Canada, Ottawa.

Wright, James V., William E. Taylor, Roscoe Wilmeth, and William N. Irving
1210. 1969 "Canada before Cartier". In, *The Canada Year Book for 1968*, Dominion Bureau of Statistics, pp. 3-11.

Wyman, Jeffries
1211. 1875 "Fresh-water shell mounds of the St. Johns River, Florida". *Peabody Academy of Science, Memoirs*, No. 4, Salem.

Yeatman, Harry C.
1212. 1964 "Surface material from Maury County, Tennessee". *Tennessee Archaeologist*, Vol. 20, No. 2, pp. 59-79.

Young, Bennett H.
1213. 1910 "The prehistoric men of Kentucky". *Filson Club Publication*, No. 25, Louisville.

Addenda

Antevs, Ernst
1214. 1937 "The age of 'Minnesota man'". *Carnegie Institute of Washington Yearbook,* No. 36, pp. 335-338.

Benthall, Joseph L., and Ben C. McCary
1215. 1973 "The Williamson Site: A new approach". *Archaeology of Eastern North America,* Vol. 1, No. 1, pp. 127-132.

Broyles, B.J.
1216. 1966 "Excavations at the St. Albans Archaic site, 1964-65". *Eastern States Archaeological Federation, Bulletin,* No. 25.

1217. 1968 "St. Albans Archaic site, West Virginia". *West Virginia Geological Survey, Newsletter,* 11th issue, 15 pp.

Bryan, Alan Lyle
1218. 1965 "Paleo-American prehistory". *Idaho State University Museum, Occasional Papers,* No. 16, Pocatello, Idaho.

Burmaster, E.R.
1219. 1932 "Reports of archaeological field work in North America during 1931". *American Anthropologist,* Vol. 34, No. 3, p. 491.

Cunningham, Roger M.
1220. 1973 "Paleo-hunters along the Ohio River". *Archaeology of Eastern North America,* Vol. 1, No. 1, pp. 118-126.

Dragoo, Don W.
1221. 1973 "Wells Creek—An Early Man site in Stewart County, Tennessee". *Archaeology of Eastern North America,* Vol. 1, No. 1, pp. 1-56.

Galbreath, E.C.
1222. 1938 "Post glacial fossil vertebrates from east-central Illinois". *Field Museum of Natural History, Geological Series,* Vol. 6, No. 20, Chicago pp. 303-313.

Gardner, William M.
1223. 1973 "Some thoughts concerning Paleo-Indians in the eastern Woodlands, including a proposed model based on excavations at the Thunderbird Site". Abstract, *Eastern States Archeological Federation, Bulletin,* No. 32, p. 11.

Gross, Hugo
1224. 1951 "Mastodons, mammoths and man in America". *Texas Archeological and Paleontological Society,* Vol. 22, Lubbock, pp. 101-131.

Haag, William G.
1225. 1942 "Early horizons in the southeast". *American Antiquity*, Vol. 7, No. 3, pp. 209-222.

Holmquist, June Drenning, and Jean A. Brookins
1226. 1972 (Second Edition) *Minnesota's major historic sites: A guide.* Minnesota Historical Society, St. Paul.

Hooton, Earnest A.
1227. 1946 (Revised Edition) *Up from the ape.* Macmillan and Company, New York.

Irving, William N.
1228. 1968 "The barren grounds". In, *Science, history, and Hudson Bay*, C.S. Beals (Editor). Department of Energy, Mines and Resources, Ottawa, pp. 26-54.

Jenks, Albert E., and Lloyd A. Wilford
1229. 1938 "The Sauk Valley skeleton". *Texas Archeological and Paleontological Society, Bulletin*, Vol. 10, Abilene, pp. 136-139.

Kapp, Ronald O.
1230. 1970 "A 24,000-year-old Jefferson mammoth from Midland County, Michigan". *Michigan Academician*, Vol. III, No. 2, Papers of the Michigan Academy of Sciences, Arts, and Letters, pp. 95-100.

Koch, A.C.
1231. 1860a Remarks in "Journal of proceedings for April 5, 1858", *Transactions of the Academy of Science of St. Louis*, Vol. 1, pp. 117-118.

1232. 1860b "Mastodon remains, in the State of Missouri, together with evidence of the existence of man contemporaneously with the mastodon". *Transactions of the Academy of Science of St. Louis*, Vol. 1, pp. 61-64.

Kraft, Herbert C.
1233. 1973 "The Plenge Site: A Paleo-Indian occupation site in New Jersey". *Archaeology of Eastern North America*, Vol. 1, No. 1, pp. 56-117.

Leverett, Frank, and Frederick W. Sardeson
1234. 1932 "Quaternary geology of Minnesota and parts of adjacent states". *United States Geological Survey, Professional Paper* 161, pp. 119-146.

Montagu, M.F.A., and C.B. Peterson
1235. 1944 "The earliest account of the association of human artifacts with fossil mammals in North America". *Proceedings of the American Philosophical Society*, Vol. 87, No. 5, Philadelphia, pp. 407-419.

Neuman, Robert W.
1236. 1966 Review of, *Paleo-American prehistory*, by A.L. Bryan, 1965. In, *Plains Anthropologist*, Vol. 11, No. 33, pp. 231-232.

Putnam, F.W.
1237. 1885 "Man and the mastodon". *Science*, Vol. 6, No. 143, pp. 375-376.

Richards Horace G.
1238. 1951 "The vindication of Natchez man". *Frontiers*, Vol. 15, No. 5, Philadelphia Academy of Natural Sciences, pp. 139-140.

Rouse, Irving
1239. 1951 "A survey of Indian River archaeology, Florida". *Yale University Publications in Anthropology*, No. 44.

Sanford, John T.
1240. 1935 "The Richmond mastodon". *Proceedings of the Rochester Academy of Science*, Vol. 7, No. 5, pp. 135-156.

Schmitt, Karl
1241. 1952 "Archeological chronology of the middle Atlantic states". In, *Archeology of eastern United States*, James B. Griffin (Editor), University of Chicago Press, Chicago, pp. 59-70.

Willey, Gordon R., and Philip Phillips
1242. 1962 *Method and theory in American archaeology*. Phoenix Books, University of Chicago Press.

Geographical Index

CANADA

New Brunswick: 745.

Newfoundland and Labrador: 437, 1076, 1077.

Nova Scotia: 85, 147, 148, 704, 706, 992, 1072, 1073.

Ontario: 58, 95, 210, 234, 309, 310, 311, 345, 346, 347, 348, 349, 350, 351, 352, 357, 359, 360, 413, 502, 534, 560, 563, 564, 600, 601, 602, 603, 604, 605, 606, 607, 608, 609, 612, 613, 614, 615, 616, 714, 752, 934, 994, 995, 999, 1067, 1069, 1070, 1071, 1206, 1207, 1209.

Prince Edward Island: —

Quebec: 330, 610, 695, 723, 724, 725, 726, 969, 1077.

UNITED STATES

Alabama: 107, 113, 134, 155, 156, 158, 159, 160, 161, 193, 204, 205, 206, 207, 208, 230, 267, 274, 380, 383, 410, 473, 474, 500, 536, 539, 544, 545, 546, 548, 549, 550, 551, 553, 555, 570, 611, 636, 672, 683, 684, 687, 688, 689, 715, 716, 717, 719, 807, 808, 809, 810, 813, 814, 829, 966, 1038, 1052, 1053, 1058, 1086, 1123, 1124, 1133, 1134, 1146.

Arkansas: 823, 824, 825.

Connecticut: 700, 755, 885, 888, 984.

Delaware: 18, 199, 858, 1081, 1142.

Florida: 14, 79, 106, 124, 125, 126, 127, 128, 129, 130, 131, 171, 172, 184, 185, 186, 187, 188, 268, 314, 315, 316, 317, 318, 319, 320, 321, 322, 323, 332, 334, 335, 336, 337, 338, 373, 374, 414, 416, 417, 418, 419, 422, 423, 424, 425, 441, 471, 472, 485, 493, 494, 495, 526, 556, 623, 692, 693, 694, 701, 702, 744, 796, 837, 838, 839, 841, 843, 844, 845, 846, 847, 857, 979, 980, 983, 1004, 1005, 1006, 1007, 1008, 1009, 1010, 1011, 1012, 1013, 1024, 1025, 1026, 1027, 1028, 1029, 1060, 1061, 1062, 1095, 1113, 1114, 1115, 1116, 1118, 1119, 1120, 1121, 1128, 1137, 1138, 1211, 1239.

Georgia: 152, 153, 243, 720, 721, 861, 1126, 1179.

Illinois: 53, 72, 73, 74, 75, 211, 275, 276, 277, 278, 279, 312, 371, 442, 444, 454, 598, 618, 743, 834, 835, 836, 869, 1082, 1094, 1100, 1164, 1165, 1222.

Indiana: 221, 236, 339, 452, 860.

Kentucky: 94, 229, 271, 398, 450, 509, 528, 698, 741, 863, 970, 971, 972, 1129, 1130, 1178, 1213.

Louisiana: 232, 306, 307, 308, 1127.

Maine: 149, 408.

Maryland: 212, 219, 220, 467, 1055.

Massachusetts: 123, 139, 140, 141, 142, 143, 145, 191, 239, 267, 283, 284, 291, 292, 376, 818, 954, 955, 956, 1018.

Michigan: 22, 23, 24, 64, 65, 83, 115, 168, 178, 209, 212, 213, 214, 244, 246, 247, 250, 251, 252, 253, 255, 262, 263, 326, 327, 328, 341, 342, 343, 440, 448, 705, 735, 876, 877, 878, 883, 891, 892, 931, 932, 974, 976, 1031, 1064, 1101, 1102, 1103, 1104, 1105, 1106, 1107, 1108, 1109, 1110, 1111, 1177, 1230.

Minnesota: 17, 56, 57, 59, 60, 61, 62, 104, 117, 120, 121, 150, 151, 203, 265, 435, 436, 439, 455, 464, 488, 497, 515, 516, 518, 519, 520, 521, 522, 523, 524, 525, 529, 558, 569, 589, 590, 591, 722, 890, 929, 985, 996, 1021, 1059, 1065, 1078, 1079, 1088, 1089, 1091, 1092, 1139, 1140, 1141, 1161, 1214, 1226, 1227, 1229, 1234.

Mississippi: 96, 109, 216, 306, 307, 411, 716, 819, 919, 1063, 1238.

Missouri: 55, 200, 576, 577, 1032, 1231, 1232.

New Hampshire: 249, 480.

New Jersey: 4, 5, 28, 29, 30, 31, 32, 33, 34, 35, 38, 39, 40, 43, 44, 45, 46, 122, 162, 196, 197, 198, 199, 218, 331, 420, 433, 458, 459, 460, 462, 471, 489, 575, 578, 593, 625, 626, 794, 868, 871, 872, 913, 933, 988, 991, 1056, 1057, 1099, 1154, 1159, 1167, 1189, 1199, 1200, 1202, 1222, 1233, 1241.

New York: 7, 25, 27, 54, 69, 98, 99, 100, 101, 103, 174, 175, 176, 183, 237, 296, 298, 299, 300, 301, 302, 303, 304, 324, 376, 377, 382, 412, 620, 925, 926, 935, 937, 943, 944, 946, 947, 948, 1000, 1047, 1084, 1093.

North Carolina: 20, 88, 89, 91, 92, 180, 181, 182, 188, 189, 404, 648, 756, 761, 804, 812, 1085.

Ohio: 6, 9, 10, 12, 21, 50, 63, 81, 84, 96, 108, 111, 163, 164, 177, 223, 242, 378, 426, 434, 466, 487, 532, 559, 599, 621, 622, 691, 815, 816, 817, 820, 822, 827, 828, 854, 855, 864, 873, 882, 886, 894, 895, 897, 898, 899, 901, 903, 904, 906, 908, 909, 910, 911, 912, 930, 1020, 1022, 1030, 1033, 1034, 1035, 1036, 1037, 1042, 1043, 1045, 1046, 1097, 1190, 1191, 1192, 1193, 1196, 1197, 1198, 1216.

Pennsylvania: 77, 78, 216, 219, 245, 379, 467, 486, 565, 566, 567, 568, 595, 596, 597, 628, 727, 732, 733, 788, 790, 800, 986, 1168, 1169, 1170, 1171.

Rhode Island: 280, 287.

South Carolina: 152, 153, 181, 182, 801, 802, 803, 842, 1098, 1117, 1125.

Tennessee: 15, 132, 158, 224, 226, 227, 248, 273, 375, 384, 385, 386, 387, 388, 389, 390, 391, 392, 393, 394, 395, 396, 397, 399, 400, 401, 402, 403, 405, 406, 407, 438, 449, 450, 537, 539, 546, 552, 572, 573, 574, 631, 633, 634, 635, 637, 640, 641, 642, 643, 644, 645, 646, 647, 649, 650, 651, 652, 653, 654, 655, 656, 657, 658, 659, 660, 661, 662, 663, 664, 665, 666, 667, 668, 669, 670, 671, 673, 674, 675, 676, 677, 678, 679, 680, 681, 682, 685, 792, 826, 856, 863, 875, 905, 1039, 1041, 1048, 1054, 1074, 1083, 1132, 1148, 1212, 1217, 1221.

Vermont: 66, 938.

Virginia: 1, 87, 90, 93, 135, 136, 257, 325, 449, 456, 457, 467, 561, 562, 629, 699, 753, 754, 758, 759, 760, 762, 763, 764, 765, 766, 767, 769, 770, 771, 772, 773, 774, 775, 776, 777, 778, 779, 780, 781, 782, 783, 804, 806, 812, 862, 874, 879, 880, 887, 893, 960, 967, 1143, 1215, 1216, 1217, 1240.

West Virginia: 47, 114, 624, 686, 787, 870.

Wisconsin: 138, 217, 237, 305, 501, 740, 742, 850, 851, 884, 950, 951, 952, 953, 993, 1066, 1074, 1162, 1205.

Index of Selected Topics

Artifacts from mid-Wisconsinan deposits or earlier: 835, 925, 978.

Bibliographies: 94, 105, 545, 560, 892, 1012, 1014, 1015.

Browns Valley man, Minnesota: (see human skeletal remains).

Faunal-Early Man associations (see also Dutchess Quarry Cave and Holcombe sites; bone and ivory tools; faunal extinction; Lenape stone; Middle Mississippi refuse pits with mastodon bones):
bison: 237, 1021.

    caribou: 178, 179, 183, 263, 298, 303, 376, 377.

    mammoth: 184, 314, 317, 341, 342, 343, 431, 595, 692, 927.

    mammoth and/or mastodon: 7, 16, 174, 175, 533.

    mastodon: 3, 49, 55, 176, 197, 198, 200, 215, 235, 238, 576, 577, 819, 859, 919, 1016, 1080, 1148, 1177, 1219, 1222, 1224, 1231, 1232, 1235, 1237, 1238, 1240, 1241.

    miscellaneous: 469, 472, 510, 696, 815, 840, 857, 973, 1004, 1005, 1008, 1024, 1138, 1156.

Faunal extinction: 233, 234, 238, 445, 446, 447, 448, 510, 579, 711, 728, 729, 730, 739, 902, 907, 1145, 1148.

Fluting techniques: (see projectile point fluting and other manufacturing techniques)

Guides to the identification of Palaeo-Indian projectile point types and miscellaneous typological studies and comments (see also projectile point fluting and other manufacturing techniques): 71, 93, 106, 108, 125, 127, 157, 160, 182, 246, 247, 254, 255, 256, 257, 281, 282, 283, 284, 286, 288, 292, 295, 327, 380, 385, 487, 505, 507, 539, 540, 541, 542, 543, 544, 547, 573, 580, 581, 583, 611, 619, 632, 636, 637, 639, 640, 641, 650, 684, 706, 722, 734, 735, 739, 740, 742, 751, 757, 758, 765, 766, 783, 801, 824, 829, 839, 840, 842, 844, 854, 885, 890, 905, 909, 943, 947, 952, 972, 976, 977, 989, 1053, 1066, 1111, 1149, 1171, 1172, 1180.

Human skeletal remains: 2, 56, 57, 83, 117, 120, 121, 171, 172, 185, 186, 203, 215, 231, 314, 315, 316, 318, 319, 320, 321, 322, 323, 326, 414, 417, 418, 419, 421, 425, 455, 488, 489, 490, 491, 492, 493, 494, 495, 496, 497, 498, 499, 515, 516, 518, 519, 520, 521, 522, 523, 524, 525, 558, 617, 693, 694, 711, 742, 744, 819, 871, 872, 913, 914, 919, 929, 979, 980, 985, 988, 1004, 1005, 1006, 1007, 1008, 1009, 1010, 1012, 1013, 1014, 1015, 1060, 1061, 1062, 1063, 1092, 1095, 1180, 1214, 1226, 1227, 1229, 1234, 1239.

Lenape stone: 595, 788.

Lively complex (see also Palaeo-Indian antecedents): 133, 134, 207, 456, 473, 474, 500, 545, 546, 548, 550, 551, 552, 687, 688, 689, 719, 966, 1087, 1132, 1133.

Middle Mississippi refuse pits containing mastodon bones: 49.

Minnesota man: (see human skeletal remains).

Miscellaneous artifacts:
- argillite implements from New Jersey: 218, 433, 739, 1167.
- bone and ivory tools:
    - mammoth: 130.
    - mammoth or mastodon: 526.
    - mastodon: 19, 629, 880.
    - other: 810.
- burins: 242, 806.
- cody knives: 54.
- Folsom flakes: 630.
- gravers and artifacts with graver spurs (see also various site reports): 274, 325, 333, 671, 678, 850, 851, 951.
- ground stone: 843.
- hafted flake knives: 1115
- Lamellar blades: 107, 1065, 1173.
- re-worked artifacts: 295, 409, 536, 647, 901.

Old Quartz industry, Georgia and South Carolina: 153, 154.

Old World-New World cultural relationships during the late Pleistocene (see also Palaeo-Indian antecedents): 116, 350, 353, 354, 356, 431, 506, 513, 514, 527, 562, 588, 710, 711, 832, 833, 1145, 1218.

Palaeo-Indian antecedents (includes reports of "Eolithic" and "Palaeolithic" tools and pebble tools; see also: artifacts from mid-Wisconsinan deposits or earlier; Lively complex; Old World-New World cultural relationships during the late Pleistocene): 4, 5, 6, 9, 12, 17, 27, 28, 29, 30, 31, 32, 33, 34, 35, 36, 37, 38, 39, 40, 41, 42, 43, 44, 45, 46, 53, 59, 60, 61, 62, 64, 65, 67, 77, 78, 81, 102, 133, 134, 162, 164, 166, 167, 194, 195, 196, 197, 198, 207, 218, 230, 240, 324, 339, 353, 428, 430, 432, 433, 434, 435, 436, 442, 458, 459, 460, 462, 463, 464, 465, 466, 467, 468, 469, 470, 471, 472, 473, 474, 494, 500, 546, 548, 549, 550, 551, 552, 559, 561, 562, 571, 587, 588, 593, 597, 600, 601, 602, 603, 604, 605, 606, 609, 613, 615, 616, 625, 626, 627, 628, 687, 688, 689, 690, 696, 697, 708, 709, 710, 711, 736, 739, 745, 784, 785, 786, 789, 790, 791, 793, 794, 816, 835, 868, 873, 889, 914, 915, 916, 917, 925, 927, 933, 966, 978, 990, 991, 994, 995, 1017, 1023, 1056, 1057, 1084, 1087, 1088, 1089, 1099, 1132, 1133, 1145, 1150, 1155, 1167, 1189, 1190, 1191, 1192, 1193, 1194, 1195, 1196, 1197, 1198, 1199, 1200, 1202, 1203, 1218.

Pleistocene beaches in the Great Lakes region and Palaeo-Indian occupation: 58, 64, 221, 262, 263, 352, 360, 476, 477, 478, 589, 604, 714, 735, 738, 739, 742, 909, 920, 921, 923, 924, 944, 946, 994, 995, 1036, 1037, 1067, 1068, 1070, 1209.

Pleistocene fauna, selected miscellaneous studies (see also faunal-Early Man associations; faunal extinctions):

bison: 237.

mammoth: 25, 168, 236, 598, 1031, 1097, 1109, 1221, 1230.

mastodon: 25, 84, 176, 233, 234, 235, 236, 378, 412, 426, 440, 598, 698, 1031, 1080.

other: 110, 185, 187, 415, 416, 422, 423, 424, 448, 510, 528, 729, 837, 869, 973, 999, 1011, 1025, 1026, 1027, 1028, 1131, 1136, 1137.

Projectile point fluting and other manufacturing techniques: 93, 246, 247, 254, 255, 256, 257, 380, 451, 540, 555, 583, 653, 706, 709, 734, 735, 754, 852, 862, 866, 904, 909, 976, 977, 1045, 1142, 1205.

Quarries: 360, 461, 467, 565, 604, 609, 789, 790, 1143.

Radiocarbon dates (see also faunal extinctions): 103, 143, 145, 149, 182, 193, 208, 267, 268, 276, 277, 302, 303, 365, 366, 370, 408, 427, 428, 429, 430, 431, 432, 445, 446, 512, 530, 531, 603, 604, 706, 708, 739, 743, 799, 807, 808, 946, 962, 1021, 1073, 1149, 1215.

Regional syntheses (selected): 51, 74, 102, 154, 179, 182, 228, 260, 270, 297, 361, 363, 364, 366, 367, 368, 369, 370, 371, 428, 429, 430, 431, 432, 433, 447, 492, 496, 514, 527, 531, 538, 588, 708, 710, 711, 713, 730, 731, 739, 832, 833, 895, 918, 924, 939, 940, 942, 944, 946, 949, 1003, 1016, 1144, 1145, 1147, 1149, 1150, 1180, 1181, 1218, 1242.

Sauk Valley man, Minnesota: (see human skeletal remains).

Settlement and social organization, patterns of site location, long range movements and other evidence of Palaeo-Indian adaptations (see also faunal extinctions; Pleistocene beaches in the Great Lakes region and Palaeo-Indian occupation): 68, 85, 86, 102, 154, 178, 179, 182, 258, 260, 261, 262, 263, 285, 293, 297, 298, 303, 304, 367, 368, 369, 370, 372, 447, 704, 705, 706, 708, 710, 711, 739, 751, 823, 825, 939, 940, 944, 946, 949, 970, 971, 972, 1003, 1016, 1021, 1064, 1068, 1110, 1135, 1145, 1147, 1149, 1150, 1151, 1152, 1153, 1171, 1180, 1181.

Trenton, New Jersey human remains: (see human skeletal remains).

Vero human remains, Florida: (see human skeletal remains).

Index of Selected Sites and Localities

Abbott Farm, New Jersey: 196, 197, 198, 933.

Asbury Rock House Site, Alabama: 206.

Barnes Site, Michigan: 1205.

Big Bone Cave, Tennessee: 438.

Boats Site, Massachusetts: 291.

Bolen Bluff, Florida: 124.

Brewerton, New York: 935.

Brohm Site, Ontario: 607, 614, 714, 1209.

Bull Brook, Massachusetts: 139, 140, 141, 142, 143, 145, 239, 267, 294, 1172.

Camp Creek Site, Tennessee: 657.

Carlson Annis Mound 5, Kentucky: 1129.

Davis Site, New York: 944, 946.

Debert Site, Nova Scotia: 147, 148, 704, 706, 992, 1072, 1073.

Delaware Valley: 4, 5, 28, 29, 30, 31, 32, 33, 34, 35, 38, 39, 40, 43, 44, 45, 46, 162, 194, 195, 196, 420, 433, 458, 549, 460, 462, 468, 471, 489, 491, 571, 575, 593, 620, 625, 626, 627, 628, 736, 737, 789, 791, 793, 794, 868, 871, 872, 889, 913, 916, 917, 933, 988, 991, 1017, 1056, 1057, 1096, 1099, 1154, 1159, 1167, 1187, 1188, 1189, 1199, 1200, 1201, 1202.

Dutchess Quarry Cave, New York: 99, 183, 298, 301, 302, 303, 377.

Ellsworth Falls, Maine: 149, 408.

Fish Creek Site, Florida: 556.

Flint Creek Rockshelter, Alabama: 161.

Flint Run Jasper Quarry, Virginia: 1143.

Flooded Cave, Florida: 268.

Fowl Lakes, Michigan: 883.

George Lake Sites, Ontario: 349, 350, 352, 357, 360.

Havey Site, Wisconsin: 850, 851.

Hi-Lo, Michigan: 251, 253, 328.

Holcombe Sites, Michigan: 22, 23, 24, 178, 179, 212, 213, 214, 255, 263, 705, 1064, 1102, 1103, 1104, 1105, 1106, 1107, 1108, 1110, 1111.

Honey Run Site, Ohio: 882.

Horseleg Mountain, Georgia: 720.

Island 35 Mastodon, Tennessee: 1148.

Isle of Wight, Virginia: 874.

Itasca Bison Kill Site, Minnesota: 1021.

Johnson Mill Rockshelter, Virginia: 767.

Keiser Site, Ohio: 828.

Kentucky Lake, Tennessee: 656, 658, 659, 675.

Kings Road Site, New York: 304.

Koster Site, Illinois: 1082.

Kouba Site, Wisconsin: 950, 951.

Kralosky Site, Michigan: 244.

Le Croy Site, Tennessee: 645, 651.

Little Falls, Minnesota: 60, 61, 62, 1088, 1089, 1091.

McConnell Site, Ohio: 904.

McKibben Site, Ohio: 912.

Melbourne, Florida: (see Vero, Florida).

Modoc Rock Shelter, Illinois: 277, 278, 279.

Mud Valley Site, Ohio: 906.

Nalcrest, Florida: 129.

Natchez, Mississippi: 215, 819, 919, 1063, 1156.

Nebo Hill, Alabama: 509, 829.

New Paris No. 4, Pennsylvania: 379.

Nuckolls Site, Tennessee: 622, 673.

Ohio Valley: 222, 225, 381, 505, 746, 747, 748, 749, 750, 1220.

Paint Rock River Site, Alabama: 683.

Parches Cave Site, Alabama: 683.

Parrish Village Site, Kentucky: 1130.

Pickett Site, Tennessee: 680.

Pinellas Point, Florida: 332.

Pine Tree Site, Alabama: 156, 158.

Plenge, New Jersey: 578, 1222, 1233.

Potts Site, New York: 944, 946.

Quad Site, Alabama: 160, 1052, 1053.

Raddatz Rockshelter, Wisconsin: 268, 1176.

Raisch-Smith Site, Ohio: 817.

Rappuhun mastodon, Michigan: 1177.

Reagen Site, Vermont: 938.

Renier Site, Wisconsin: 742.

Richmond, Virginia: 87.

Russell Cave, Alabama: 113, 193, 267, 807, 808, 809, 810, 813, 814.

Saltville, Virginia: 90.

Savage Cave, Kentucky: 230.

Sawmill Site, Ohio: 1042.

Sheep Rock Shelter, Pennsylvania: 799.

Sheguiandah, Ontario: 210, 600, 601, 602, 603, 604, 605, 606, 608, 609, 612, 613, 615, 616, 994, 995, 1209.

Shoop, Pennsylvania: 1171, 1172.

Silver Springs, Florida: 838.

Stanfield-Worley, Alabama: 205, 208, 383.

St. Albans, Virginia: 1216, 1217.

Stone Pipe Site, Alabama: 155.

Taylor Site, South Carolina: 803.

Timlin Site, New York: 27, 1084.

Tolles Site, Michigan: 878.

Trenton, New Jersey: (see Delaware Valley).

Trilisa Pond Site, Florida: 841.

Twin Rivers Site, Rhode Island: 280, 287.

Vero and/or Melbourne, Florida: 79, 171, 172, 185, 186, 314, 315, 316, 317, 318, 319, 320, 321, 322, 323, 414, 415, 416, 417, 418, 419, 423, 425, 471, 472, 493, 494, 495, 496, 499, 692, 693, 694, 701, 702, 744, 745, 845, 979, 980, 1004, 1005, 1006, 1007, 1008, 1009, 1010, 1012, 1013, 1060, 1061, 1062, 1063, 1095, 1137, 1138, 1239.

Wakulla Cave, Florida: 857.

Wapanucket No. 8, Massachusetts: 954, 955, 956.

Wells Creek Crater, Tennessee: 224, 227, 1217, 1221.

Welti Site, Michigan: 252.

West Athens Hill Site, New York: 296.

Williamson Site, Virginia: 76, 325, 765, 766, 769, 772, 783, 1215.

Z
1208
N6
S77

FEB 3 1976